A TIME REMEMBERED

A Time Remembered

Richard Walker

Gomer Press
1987

First publication — May 1987

ISBN 0 86383 310 1

Printed by J. D. Lewis & Sons.,
Gomer Press, Llandysul, Dyfed

For Molly
and Helen and Sarah

I dedicate this book to the villagers of
Capel Newydd, especially Eirlys and
Megan. And to the memory of
Mr and Mrs Llewellyn Thomas and
Muriel, and the others who have
passed on, for they all enriched
my life.

1

The little church still stands in isolation on its triangle of littered grass, bypassed on all sides by Hythe's traffic. At one time its corrugated iron roof and sides were coloured in various hues of green, and grime cast dark fingers over its plain windows. The railings were bent and curved, and the path overgrown with weeds. It still stands in the middle of its little island, now a dirty white, a legacy of Victorian parsimony.

In 1939 I was a choirboy here. Surpliced and cassocked I floated, angel-like, with my friends up the centre aisle, hands clasped round my hymnal, and I filed off to the left and took my place in front of the choir stalls, singing all the time in weak soprano. The Tin Church, as it was known, was homely and warm, with deep-red pine pews, red carpeted floor, and a vestry with tall cupboards and hissing radiators. As choristers, we were paid sixpence a week, sufficient for two comics and a sherbet.

It was here, in this quaint, homely place of worship, that my war began, for at eleven o'clock on the morning of September 3rd, 1939, as the service began, a siren wailed. In a troubled voice our vicar explained that we were now at war with Germany, and God help us all. Terror touched me. I wanted to flee the church, go home, hide in my bedroom. But we sang on, and I recall no more of that day.

That period is referred to as the Phoney War, but to us children it was the Funny War. We had never seen such urgency, heard so much noise, been so much shoved aside and herded along. We all trooped down to the World's Smallest Railway by Hythe Canal—already isolated by rolls of barbed wire—to be fitted with gasmasks and we made pig noises to each other through the soft rubber. We waved at the odd German plane that droned along the seafront, and at the planeloads of refugees from Europe that came low over our playing area to land at Lympne on the brow of the Roughs, just three miles away. We waved at the School of Musketry as they went to war, and we waved at the Black Watch Regiment as it bag-piped its way with magnificent arrogance down Dymchurch

Road. We waved at friend and foe alike enjoying, in our complete innocence, the play and the costumes of the Phoney War.

Our parents went to numerous War Lectures, given by solemn men from the Ministry of Defence. They learned how to erect Anderson and Morrison shelters and what to do when the enemy began bombing, and what measures to take if the gas clouds rolled in. Suddenly, old people (in their forties and fifties) seemed to sprout up at road junctions, brandishing Lee Enfields, and we giggled at their forage caps and gaiters.

The harshest thing of all was the total blackout. Wardens on their tall black bikes came around the streets yelling 'Blackout!' or 'Put that light out!'. When winter came, the darkness was something new to us, unfriendly and solid. I remember running to post a letter one evening and crashing straight into the letter box, suffering a deep gash and a bloodied nose. There were similar accidents all the time. Schooldays, however, were unchanging. We gathered on the Green in loud groups and then, when the whistle blew, formed ranks and marched across the road and into school to the tap of a drum played by a senior boy. The only difference was that we now carried gasmasks wherever we went. Our teachers did not discuss the war with us.

We also tolerated, and even played with, the London evacuees. They must have been deposited on us in error, for they did not stay long. We decided then that evacuees had snotty noses, smelled rather like old wash-flannels, wore their jacket sleeves too short and their trousers too long, had a penchant for red, white and blue snake belts, and threw stones and kicked tins along the gutters. At first, we viewed them with the unreasonable hostility that children can show towards each other, but feelings on both sides neutralised before long. It was the first time that we had shared our secret paths and special trees with strangers.

Our part of Kent had lost its special rural appeal within months of war being declared. Army Camps sprang up in the woods, gun sites pocked the holy acres of the Golf Club, the seafront was mined and barbwired, hotels were requisitioned, and nearly every garden was planted with an Anderson Shelter.

8

But before the situation became too strained, we went to Wales as evacuees ourselves. Parcelled and labelled, we waved to our weeping parents with glee as the crammed steam engine puffed out of Sandling Junction, bound non-stop for far off Pembrokeshire. For a while, especially towards the end of the journey, war was not much fun, for we had run out of jokes and conversation and felt grimy and cramped. I remember my toothache beginning, and one of the teachers shoving a piece of cotton wool soaked in iodine into the cavity.

It was late in the evening of June 23rd, 1940, when we arrived at Crymych, our destination, and were gently herded by complete strangers into the large drill hall there, where ladies with kind faces and sing-song voices drifted amongst us with cups of hot tea and delicious Welsh cakes, to which I soon became addicted. Our numbers gradually diminished as we were selected by our hosts and taken away to new homes. A fine looking old man in tweeds and plus fours, with a red face and white moustache and kind, wrinkled eyes, approached us with our headmaster. 'Boys,' said our headmaster, 'this is Mr Daniel Daniels. He has very kindly offered to take five boys and Mrs Hawkins and me into his home. Now, I want Eric Turner, Ronald Baker, David Reeves, Dick Walker and Malcolm Saunders to pick up your cases and come with us'.

And so we began the last stage of the journey to our new life, in the back of a splendid station wagon that seemed to be made as much of wood as of metal. Odd as it may seem, it was the first time I had ever been in a real car—I had only sat in a Rolls Royce before this. We boys all knew each other, but were not particular friends. David, hair bleached almost white by the sun and full of nervous energy, had invented his own language, which he rattled off to anyone who cared to listen. While doing so he would give little jumps in the air and wave his arms about. I remember that 'I' was 'Idee Pide' and 'No' was 'Noady Poad', and that it took him ages to say the simplest words. Eric was sharp featured, with a face remarkably like a young Erasmus. He leaned slightly forward when he walked, as if into his own private gale. He was the tallest of us by an inch or so. Ron was the smallest, known, rather unkindly perhaps, as Log. He was certainly the best looking, with bold dark eyes and strong, square chin, and an air of bravado about him that more

9

than made up for his lack of inches, and he was probably the brightest of us. Malcolm was upright and smart, a fine runner, who fancied himself a bit, and not without cause for he, too, was handsome in a brooding way. I was the only with curly hair and skinny legs, and was a compulsive show-off. One could say that we were a mixed bunch. I used to wonder what Daniel Daniels, Esquire, thought of us on that first encounter.

2

Ffynone Mansion reclined elegantly on the side of a wooded valley, its paved terrace poised over the beech-studded fields that swept down to the valley. The approach was through tall iron gates, along a drive that wound its way for one third of a mile in slow curves between cascading rhododendron bushes. The sky seemed to be brushed by the magnificent elms and beeches. The drive terminated in a circle of gravel, at the bottom of the broad steps of the mansion entrance, then it petered out gradually between the supports of an encircling wall, along by the domestic wing, round a corner, under an arch and into a cobbled yard, flanked by stables.

The headmaster and Mrs Hawkins arrived as we stood amidst our cases and cardboard gasmask boxes in the entrance to the domestic wing, gazing about us at the shiny cream walls and long, slippery mansion-polished floors. Daniel Daniels, Esquire, Gentleman, now introduced us to his sister, Miss Daniels, his cousin Mrs Bickerton-Edwards, Margaret the housekeeper, Mr Dunne the butler, Betty, Myfanwy and Megan the maids, all examining with interest and amusement the flotsam that had been deposited on their doorstep.

While we were being crushed by euphoric welcomings and hustled into the great kitchen, two of our party from the train had arrived a mile and a half away, at a small farm. The yard was a sea of mud, nettles festooned all the outer walls, and the man of the place seemed to be a hard character, not much interested in bestowing the comforts of home on children. Their bedroom ceiling bulged and cracked with the weight of trapped water, the ancient wallpaper peeling from the walls. It was as if the room, the farmhouse itself, had been left to the pigeons and bats for years. The two boys were frightened, lonely, and very homesick. In despair, they climbed through the bedroom window and dropped down into the orchard, and made a dash for the village and the sanctuary of our teacher's new lodgings. Mr Hummerstone had barely sat down before Roy and Desmond appeared in some distress before him. He promptly took them back to the farm, where explanations were made on both sides, and there they stayed, and life was not too bad during the following weeks and months.

Meanwhile, at the mansion, we had been seated along a massive kitchen table for a late supper, then bathed and settled into our bedrooms; David and I were in one, Ron, Malcolm and Eric in the other. I can remember quivering with excitement at the thought that we were in a real mansion, with maids and butlers and really posh people. It was better than anything I had read about.

Ffynone farm was only five minutes' walk up a rough path through a damp copse. We drifted into it quietly that first morning, in a tight, shy bunch, wary of the busy men in brown corduroys, cloth caps and white, collarless shirts and jackets with drooping pockets. We edged slowly, Indian style, round the unfamiliar buildings, side-stepping the puddles, sniffing the odours of hay and straw, cattle-cake and corn, cow-pats and horse dung, and the awful stench of the pigs.

It was not an immaculate farm as one would expect, belonging to a great house, but it was an alive farm, full of free-ranging fat hens and strutting cockerels, almost empty haggards, waggons waiting patiently in their open sheds, and a fine herd of cattle. There was a carpenter and a bailiff, three men to run the horses, a cowman, two Italian prisoners-of-war, and one or two odd farm labourers. The haggard attracted us from the very first, and this became our secret headquarters, where we sat in the sweet smelling hay and discussed all manner of important business. We were entranced by the waggons and gambos too, never having seen such vehicles before.

Although we were impressed by so much around us on that first morning, I recall most vividly the four great carthorses. They were in their stalls, towering above all living things— noble heads with gentle eyes, nostrils blowing warm breath, champing jaws, great feathered feet and swishing tails. They

11

exuded immense power. Initially, we peered at them from behind the stalls, then we reached out and laid a finger on a muscle, and the splendid beasts turned their heads and looked down at us with patient interest. They were named Bloss, Diamond, Ginger and Bowler. Bloss was jet black, a mare, and I decided she was mine. The other three were bigger, being geldings, and ranged from brown-and-white to gingery brown, and they were all gentle creatures. We became very involved with them as time went by.

The pig pens faced into a filthy enclosure many yards wide, and on that first exploratory journey we ventured over a gate and stood uncertainly in the thick mud. It was as well that we went no further, for an enormous sow trotted squealing from out of a pen and charged towards us, and there was a panicky, noisy retreat by us back over the gate. We discovered later that this sow was always bad-tempered, and positively dangerous when she had a litter.

We also found our first rats, sly and slithering, appearing and disappearing magically under the debris hidden by the nettle-beds around the sheds. Some buildings were dark, with old machinery in them, others were open, and it was obvious to us that this was a paradise for the games we played, or were going to play. It did not seem that any restrictions would be imposed on us. The farm was ours.

Having satisfied our curiosity for the time being, we returned to the mansion for our first lunch, and to learn about this new home. It all seemed very promising. One of the maids said that there were ninety-three rooms including the chauffeur's quarters over the courtyard. Could we see them? All in good time.

Our kitchen was tall and wide, dominated by the great table in the centre. The floor was of polished quarry tiles, and huge windows filled the room with light. Three of us sat on one side of the table, two the other, headmaster at one end and Mrs Hawkins fifteen feet away at the other end, and there was a deal of space between us all. The maids brought in our meals from a smaller kitchen next door, and we used napkins and drank from tall glasses, and said Grace before each meal with heads bowed, headmaster intoning 'May the Lord make us truly thankful for the food we are about to receive, amen.' We were never to go hungry.

Supper seemed always to have a special quality, possibly because we never knew what it would be, and the surprise of it usually delighted us. A favourite was a piece of cold rabbit with home-made pickle, and we always had a china mug of steaming cocoa. Or there might be rissoles, sometimes fish and chips. Whatever the meal, it was never quite enough to satisfy our ravenous appetites, but it was more than enough on which to sleep after bathtime.

We had our own playroom in which to spend the indoor hours. There was the shoe-cleaning room where we had to kick off our shoes every time we entered the house, and a large, cold buttery where we helped the maids make buttermilk, Mr Dunne's pantry—only peered at but never entered, the laundry room with racks that were hauled up to the high ceiling. We had never dreamed that there could be such a diversity of rooms in one house. As yet, we had not entered the Real House—we were still only in the domestic wing.

The headmaster and Mrs Hawkins had their own living room opposite our playroom, and they retired here to leave us to our own devices. The very presence of Mr Hawkins ensured that we behaved ourselves, for he was stern. The first sign of his displeasure was a chilling stare from his blue eyes. Words were superfluous, the stare was sufficient. He was a very good tenor, and this probably endeared him to the local people from the beginning. He was always involved one way or another with music, and played the piano well. Mrs Hawkins was very quiet, but she too had only to stare to quell any disorder. We had all the freedom we needed, but we were under constant surveillance. There had to be a price to pay for this splendid new life. When we went to bed, Mrs Hawkins came round to tuck us up and put out the lights and bid us sleep well. She was rather like a mother.

School in the tiny village of Capel Newydd, a mile and a bit up the road from our mansion, was modest by any standards. In fact, we all attended the Llyfrgell y Sir—the Library. This was one vast room on the ground floor of the centre of a short line of three houses. The Ffynone carpenter, Mr Thomas Stiff Leg, lived in the first house, and the District Nurse lived in the third

13

one. After school, Mr Thomas Stiff Leg and Mrs Thomas y Sir—his wife—came through from their side and tidied things up and changed things round so that it became the Reading Room. This was then the social centre of the village every evening, where billiards were played, and Bar Billiards, and shove ha'penny, and Beetle and Whist Drives. The transformation was not so remarkable as adroit, because the table round which the nineteen of us studied was converted instantly into the billiard table by removing the top. All around us, stacked almost to the ceiling, were rows of chairs and small tables, card tables for the whist and beetle drives. There was also an open fire, and Mrs Thomas sometimes came in during our lessons and added coal or logs to it if the day was cold. Our teacher, Mr Hummerstone, and his wife, had the adjoining room, so he simply appeared without warning at the start of morning school. It was all very friendly, what with Mr Thomas Stiff Leg and Mrs Thomas and the Hummerstones coming and going through the same door. At one time or other most of us had a toothache or a stomach upset, and we would be settled into a comfortable chair in the Hummerstone's room, while Mrs Hummerstone spoiled us completely with sympathy and cups of tea. It was almost a pleasure being ill.

But there was another function to this remarkable room. On the first Wednesday of each month the Reading Room became the Quarter Sessions Room, whereupon we all trooped up to the village school a quarter of a mile away, to join the Welsh children, for there was nowhere else to go.

Schooling, however, was not cramped by adversity. It was strict, and the task of keeping an eye on us was made easy by its very cosiness. We lacked desks, of course, therefore there were no pet spiders, no comics, no secret paraphernalia at all. When lessons were over, all the books were piled onto a card table and covered with a cloth, and this was left in a corner of the room. Our playground was the village street, so in the mornings we hung about here in noisy, happy groups until Mrs Thomas opened up. We spilled out on to it at break and lunchtimes and at the end of the day, but there was so little traffic that it was as safe as a real playground. Indeed, if a car did happen to come along, it was such an event that we all parted and watched it pass by.

14

Each morning we came into contact with the Welsh children, who viewed us with the same disdain that we had shown the London evacuees at home. For the first few days there was only eyeballing, but this escalated before long into a mutual dislike for no reason at all other than our different circumstances. We were, after all, invaders, doubling the child population overnight.

We attended the Welsh school on our first day, and I suspect it was a public relations effort on the part of the teachers. Mr Parry, the Welsh headmaster, was small, dark and bright-eyed, with a remarkably deep voice for such a small person. Within minutes we had each been paired off with a Welsh neighbour. My new friend was Dorothy Edwards. She was at least two inches taller than me, freckled, with a lazy voice and nice eyes, and thick hair. I thought she was terrific. I would have to make her a Hurricane or something out of scrapwood.

On a blackboard had been chalked a lesson, obviously in code.

'We all of us in the British Isles sing God Save the King,' said Mr Parry in his deep voice, 'but this is our own anthem. It is about us, and it is especially ours. I would like you English children to learn it so that you can sing it on our occasions. It is called—and he spread out an arm to the blackboard—Hen Wlad fy Nhadau, Land of my Fathers.'

And so, on that bright morning, with motes suspended in the sun's rays like galaxies in space, began my love affair with Wales.

Mr Parry went on further. 'When you next come here, boys, I want to hear you say, Bore Da. That means good morning. How do you say Good Morning, now then?' And we all bellowed 'Bore Da!'

Before that first day was over I had smiled at my first Welsh girl, seen a buzzard hurtling down out of the wide sky with wings folded and cried out 'Hurricane!,' and said hello to the first one-armed person I had encountered in my eleven years of life on earth—and a jolly tramp sitting in the hedge at that.

I have no idea how the stone fights with the Welsh boys began, but it was probably due to needling on both sides— Foreigners against Funny Accents. I cannot remember the first stone cast nor the last, yet I recall vividly the two camps of

15

youngsters, the Welsh at the top of the field which had now been allocated to us for playing in, and us at the bottom, hurling abuse at each other prior to the real business of hurling stones. No one ever got hurt, but some stones came mighty close. It came to a halt when an English stone landed in the Welsh playground where the women and children were kept out of harm's way, narrowly missing—so it was said—the smallest child in the school. Teachers and headmasters were furious, culprits were lined up—certainly in our school—and given four of the best with an uncaring cane wielded by a vigorous teacher. I went back to my place at the table fighting back tears of hurt and anger, nursing throbbing fingers, uttering curses on the 'sodding Welsh.'

We saw for the first time in our lives the beauty and the labour of haymaking. It was a splendid harvest, for the weather had been fine and warm, the fields knee-deep in clover, and now it was being mown by the teams of carthorses. When the green had turned to sweet-smelling hay, the waggons creaked into the fields, and as they slowly trundled down the rows of bleached hay, the farmworkers pitchforked the hay into the waggons in great piles with unhurried, powerful movements of arms and shoulders while one or two men in the waggon strove to bed it down well in layers. We helped when we could, delighting in holding the horse's head and leading and stopping, though the horses knew exactly what to do without our help, but bore with us patiently. And as the load grew, so the task of laying it became harder, the grunts more frequent. A remembered picture still remains of the waggon swaying out of the field, pitchfork stuck in the top, and the loader, now at rest, half embedded in the hay as he held the reins of his horse. Then the next waggon to fill, and the warm air all around was scented. When we rested in the shade of a waggon, the men bantered with us. They were immensely kind and patient as they coaxed us in Welsh.

'Now then, boys, you say every morning, 'Sut mae bore ma, just like a Welshman, see? That means, how are you this morning? Let's hear you, then,'

'Shoot my boreh ma!'

'Very good, boys. Better than Mario by here.' Mario, the handsome, olive-skinned prisoner of war, grinned shyly at us.

16

We liked Mario. 'Is—a—funny language,' he said, 'like you spit—a—when you spik.'

'That's not how Mr Parry told us, Mr Jenkins,' I said.

'Mr Parry? Who's he then?' in mock surprise. Then, 'You don't take any notice of him, not if you wants to talk like us. You just listen to how we tells you, proper like, and you boys'll be talking Welsh in no time!'

And so it went on, and we picked words up and digested them like marshmallows, got our tongues round the sibilants and gutturals, and Mario and his comrade gazed across the fields and were lost in prisoner-of-war thoughts. We would subside into moments of silence, broken only by the sound of skylark and curlew, the champing of the horses with their nosebags, and an occasional stamp of a leg, the creak of shafts, the groan of a wheel as the weight shifted.

We came into contact with the Major within the first few days, smart in tweeds, middle-aged, handsome and terrific fun. He was a dynamo, and we loved him in seconds because he was one of us. With thumbstick in hand he rounded us up one Sunday afternoon.

'Shortest on the left, tallest on the right!'

We leapt yelling to his command.

'Right! Orf we go!'

We followed him down through the noble trees to the mansion garden, singing some song or other while he waved his thumbstick like a drum major. In the garden we 'fell out', were given a butterfly net each and the Major called out his orders.

'David to the left, Dick to the right, that's got rid of the fair ones, and you dark brutes go up the middle. You come with me, young Eric.'

We stalked the cabbage white butterflies all afternoon, darting amongst the plants and shrubs like children bent on intrigue, catching, squeezing, plopping the quivering white bodies into our jars. When the killing was over we tramped back to the mansion and in the kitchen the Major counted out all the bodies on a spread newspaper.

'Ninety-four! Divided by five, nineteen each at a farthing— call it fivepence each.' It was the first wage any of us had earned and the work had been so pleasurable it seemed like stealing the money.

In that first halcyon summer we walked the mile and a half to school, lunch-boxes packed, gasmask in cardboard box slung over shoulder. The air was fragrant with wild flower smells, and the humming, buzzing hedges grew right up to the blue sky and spread their multi-coloured hands out to the lanes, making them narrow and stiflingly hot. We loved the hedges more than anything else for they were another world, a secret world of winding tracks between hawthorn and elderberry and ash and sycamore, where we wove the supple young branches to form intricate barricades around snug little camps. Hedge-camps became our passsion; we excelled at them. Nothing gave us so much complete pleasure, such exhilaration, as defending our hedgecamps against the enemy. I think we must have been innovators in this new game, for there was no evidence of previous occupation by the Welsh children. We were the modern knights. When the lunch-hour bell rang we spilled out of school and hurtled the fifty yards to Cilgwyn Lane and into our camps to modify, improve, repair and extend. We defended them with swords of hazel or ash, cutting and thrusting at the enemy as they clambered up the thick-grassed slopes and tried to penetrate our fortifications. Many images flit through my mind, of a sword rattling against the cardboard guard of my own, the word Oxo still emblazoned on it, of 'Carthorse' clutching his heart and tumbling down the bank with such realism that I though he really had been mortally wounded. We had many memorable battles, our blood-curdling cries echoing down the lane and across the fields.

It was while engaged in combat that we first saw Rachel. Dead and dying lay slumped over the barricades like rag-dolls, the last few defenders were locked in fierce hand-to-hand struggles. Then Rachel appeared and we stood there, and the dying sat up, our swords were stilled as this fiery-haired creature swayed towards us down that white, dusty lane. She was tall, graceful beyond words, seventeen years old, the sun burnishing her hair and, as she passed by our scattered bodies without a glance or a word, there was not one amongst us who was not impressed by her grace. It was almost as if she were an

18

hallucination, for when the green-filled distance hid her from us, we remained stunned. Then battle resumed, and she was forgotten, but the memory remains.

Rachel's father was Mr Davies the Ffynone gamekeeper. He was a tall, silent man with piercing eyes, and always carried a shotgun under his arm. Somehow, he seemed to appear magically. When we played in the woods we would be aware that he was passing silently by, and sometimes he nodded a greeting, even smiled at us. He would appear in the courtyard, or by one of the farmsheds, a solitary hunter. He strode majestically across the skyline, or glided between the trees, and hardly a word passed between him and us. Then, one day, he came into the courtyard carrying a bundle which he passed over to Mr Hawkins. It was a buzzard. It lay limp, but still beautiful, on the rags, one leg almost torn off by the teeth of the cruel gin-trap of which it had fallen foul. There was still rage in the open eyes, a savageness about the curved beak. Mr Davies wanted us to see at close quarters what a splendid bird it was, for we might never see one this close again. We took it to school and drew it with pastels on scrap paper and measured it. From wingtip to wingtip it was precisely Ron's height—fifty inches.

We made fern camps wherever there was an acre of ferns. By trial and error we became remarkably proficient at framework fernhouses. We made three and four-roomed houses, with barricades, and camouflaged them against discovery, knowing that in a matter of a day that they would be wrecked by the Welsh boys, because we wrecked theirs and left rude notes. There was no real enmity now, but a fierce kind of pride in building things, a possessiveness, and we regarded the woods as our territory. Anyone building on our land would be prosecuted.

Before very long, most of us acquired clogs. There are many kinds of clogs—pointed, blunt, curved, straight, wooden tops, leather tops, half-covered, fully covered, with irons and without irons. But nothing compares with the Welsh clog. It is in a class of its own, possibly the most handsome footwear ever made by hand. No machinery is used in the making of a Welsh clog. It is just large enough to fit comfortably, and carved out of hewn ash blocks. The leather uppers are hand-stitched and the laces are of leather. Irons are nailed on the heel and soles, and a small tin strip on the front. I went down to Abercych one fine Saturday morning to be measured for my clogs.

Abercych clings to a mile of steep hillside in one of the loveliest areas of Pembrokeshire—Dyfed as it is now. It is a one street village, with cottages on both sides, those on the lip of the ridge about to fall into the valley, those on the opposite side about to be engulfed by the banks towering over them. The cottages are dazzling white, pretty, and the village always seemed to be busy. Here lived the clogmaker, a huge-muscled man with brown and hairless head, thick, aproned body. A genius with his hands and half-a-dozen tools. His workshop was little more than a hole in the wall, low and dark, a cavern of wood and leather smells. In one corner a pile of split logs scrambled halfway up the rock wall.

I sat on a small bench, silent, a little wary of this huge man. He beckoned me over, pulled off my wellies and placed one foot at a time on two logs, and drew the outline with chalk. In minutes, he had cut out two soles with the knife blade that swivelled on its hinge on the worn cutting block, saying not one word but emitting a series of grunts as he bent and straightened up, chopped and turned his knife round the chalklines, producing gentle curves where there had been none. Then a tape round my ankles, a few more grunts, rapid chalkmarks on each new sole that read 'D. Walker, Ffynone,' and the comment, 'Dewch 'ma next week, boyo. Five shillings.'

The Welsh clog

21

I clopped back from Abercych the following Saturday in my new clogs, feeling very tall and heavy-footed, a tin of Dubbin for my clogs in my pocket. So proud of them was I that on returning to Ffynone, I hosed them down in the courtyard, and walked round them, and gazed at them from a distance, experiencing for the first time in my life the exhilaration of ownership of an expensive item. They had cost me five shillings, even if my mother had paid for them. I left them out in the open in their puddle of water, hoping that Mr Davies the chauffeur would see them, or even Mr Daniel Daniels, Esq., Gentleman.

Everyone wore clogs, the boys and girls, women as well as men, young and old. They seemed to be the only logical footwear. One could walk through deep puddles without fear of wet feet, kick a ball higher and further, break faggots, squash rats behind the pig troughs, and even creep about in them silently once one got the knack. In summer they were cool, but in winter they were bitterly cold, like two receptacles of packed ice, and everyone stuffed them with old newspaper. And in the muddy fields they collected great balls of mud so that your knees knocked and your ankles twisted with the weight. These faults aside however, they kept your feet dry, and we became very attached to them. They were utterly reliable. All they required was a coat of Dubbin now and again, and new irons when the old ones wore thin. In four years of abusive wear I had only two pairs, and the soles of my feet became so tough that six years later I could put out the stub of a cigarette with them and not feel a thing. The clog would eventually break its back. It did not gradually die, like a boot or a shoe. One day there would be an odd feeling in the foot, perhaps after jumping a stream or kicking a stone, and that splendid ash sole would be split at the weak part, that curves up to the heel. No more sixpenny irons for these clogs, no glueing —they were finished. It was a sad moment, for we all thought our clogs were indestructable.

Among the farmworkers of Ffynone one man frightened me. Emrys was red-faced and loose-lipped and laughed maniacally at everything that went on around him, serious or otherwise.

He worked mainly with the horses, and we often saw him out in the fields ploughing with a pair, a sack around his waist, stooping over the long handles of the plough. In the tack room, Emrys would terrify us, thrusting us into dangerous situations, roaring with wet mouth at our terror. If we were combing one of the horses he would creep up and shoo the creature over against us, knowing that we could quickly duck under its belly. He also knew that the horse would think about it first, then move almost reluctantly with two small sidesteps. And once he grabbed my arm and shoved a stick in my hand, then carried me writhing to an electric wall switch with a broken cover and, dribbling with mad pleasure at my shrieks, he thrust the stick against the bare terminals. He knew a dry stick did not conduct electricity, but I didn't.

Emrys excelled himself one Saturday morning when work was finished and the men were busy doing nothing in the tack room prior to going home for the weekend. We boys had been milling around them, listening to their chatter and picking up one or two more words for our vocabularies, when Emrys suddenly grabbed me and stuffed me in a sack. Everyone, including my gang, roared encouragement. He then bade his mates 'Bore da' and carried me off, across field after field, until he came to his tied cottage. There he tipped me out on the step and disappeared inside, wet with exertion, convulsed with his mad laughter. In tears of frustration and rage I yelled at him, 'I'll get you for this, you big prick!' It was the worst language, the direst threat I could summon.

Our best friend was without question Mr Jenkins, the senior ostler. He took to us, and we to him, and he patiently and carefully taught us rudimentary Welsh, enough to make ourselves understood. We learned the familiar grammar, far enough removed from written Welsh to make it incompatible to us, but infinitely more useful. Mr Jenkins also taught us much about horses and farm matters, and the time came when he allowed us to be hoisted onto the backs of the horses one evening and ride them to their field a couple of hundred yards away. We perched on them with legs spread wide over their massive shoulders, holding a simple halter. They were led out of the yard, and we were on our own. Without prompting from us, they trotted majestically along the lane, their heads high, tails out, and we bounced helplessly from side to side on their immense backs, hanging on grimly to mane and halter. Once in their ungated field they broke into a ponderous gallop, giving their freedom kicks and making very loud rude noises; we stopped laughing for the more serious business of keeping our seats, but within seconds we had all slid under the necks. For a second longer, perhaps less, we hung on, before being tossed aside like bits of sacking, and not one great feathered hoof touched us as we bounced along the unforgiving ground.

'You didn't tell them to stop, boys,' said Mr Jenkins when he got back his breath, for he had trotted along behind us as best he could, had seen everything, and had nearly burst his ribs laughing. After a few more gasps he said, 'If you had said whoa in Welsh they might have stopped!'

Another time, we watched with interest as a proud, marvellously muscled bull was led into the field one evening, its body seemingly too big for the legs so that it appeared to be sinking as it swayed along. Without hesitation, it mounted a cow which had been brought up to it, but it missed in its thrust, and a long thin jet of semen shot along the cow's back, and both of them groaned.

'What's he doing, Mr Jenkins?' I wanted to know, in genuine innocence.

Mr Jenkins looked down at me, then at the bull and the man who controlled it, then sighed and said, 'Wel, Dick bach, you see now the cow underneath? She wants a calf, see? So that old bull on top is watering her so that the little calf will grow inside her.'

I said 'what a good idea', believing him implicitly.

Because of the effort required by every British person to do his and her utmost in helping to defeat the Germans, it was declared that summer holidays for schoolchildren would be split. They would have two weeks for the hay season, and two weeks for the corn harvest. It seemed to make sense for school during the summer was fun anyway. When we weren't in our hedgecamps, we were having piggy-back rides in our playfield. There were sufficient numbers to muster two armies of men and horses, the horses being the heavier. With a neigh and a trot we advanced towards each other, circled, then attacked. Knees often buckled at the first attack, both horse and rider collapsing to the ground in helpless mirth while the others grabbed, yelling and gyrating until there was just one big heap of twisted arms and legs in the grass, and no one ever won.

In the small adjoining field there was a stiff-legged goat with horns that swept right back over his narrow head, thus offering no danger. We sometimes crawled through the hedge and egged him on to charge us, which he obligingly did with great frequency. We allowed him to butt us, and I honestly feel that he enjoyed the game as much as we did, for his butting seemed to carry very little weight. As a reward we then handed him handfuls of dandelions, as he had grazed his small patch to baldness.

The intervening weeks between hay and corn harvesting were very lovely that first year. There are times now when I slump into the faded deckchairs of lost summers and recall the long, warm days spent in the Reading Room, with the windows open, the village sounds coming through. Life seemed so free of tension. The adults never seemed to discuss the war amongst themselves, it was as if we were on another planet, as if we had all wished the nasty things away, and only the pleasant ones remained.

Mr Parry had a small orchard, a private piece of ground which no one entered save he and his family. The only visible signs of its contents were the lush fruit hanging over the garden wall in full view of our field. I resolved to have at least one of his apples. During one break period I sped up the tiny path to the Welsh school, paused when I came to the sagging branches, leapt up and grabbed a branch for leverage and leapt higher to clutch one monstrous red apple. Then a remarkable thing happened. A flash of movement in the leaves, and the handle of a walking stick held my wrist firmly to the wall. I hung in mid

25

Mr Parry's stick pinned my arm

air, my toes barely touching the ground, my only free hand
clutching an apple.

'Got you, now then!'

The remembered voice of Mr Parry. His head appeared, and
he looked down at my stretched body, left out for the ants to
nibble away at in the heat of the midday sun. A note of triumph
enriched his deep, theatrical voice as he said, 'Ahah! Ahah!—
an English evacuee, isn't it?'

I gave him a sickly, feeble grin, unable to utter one word.

'You boys call this s-c-r-u-m-p-i-n-g, don't you?' he asked
and, without waiting for me to reply, added, 'Well, I call it
stealing! What is your name, boy?'

'Dick Walker, sir,' I whispered.

'Dick Stealer, is it then? Stealing from the people who have
given you food and shelter, and this is how you repay them?'
I could only show him the whites of my eyes, like a scolded dog,
which is how I felt.

'Right then, Dick Stealer,' he said, relinquishing his grip with the walking stick, and I thought I bet he sticks it in his belt, 'you come up to the school right away now, and don't run away, because it will only make things worse for you.'

With a sense of unreality forming a vacuum between my head and my feet, I walked up the lane and into the school playground, and as I crossed it I was aware of the curious eyes already damning me for a petty thief, and the noise of the children's play seemed to become muted, as if they were stopping everything to stare at me. Mr Parry met me at the door, and led me to a single chair in the centre of the floor. I went to sit on it, but he roared,

'No, boy! You stand on it.'

I was standing on it when the children came panting in from play and threw themselves behind their desks and looked at me, The English Apple Thief, and giggled and made rapid remarks to each other behind their hands. Mr Parry rapped his stick on a desk and said, with marvellous eloquence, 'Look you at him by there, for he is a thief, caught stealing my apples. Dick Stealer is his name, and he is an evacuee, which makes it worse. But I suppose he does not know any better.'

And so it went on. This was one of the worst moments of my life. I found the humiliation hard to bear, and tears of self pity blurred my vision. Worse, I wondered what Dorothy would think of an apple thief, and I dared not seek her out with my eyes so I stared straight ahead, feeling desolate.

I was allowed to leave eventually, almost dazed by the verbal punishment I had received, smarting with the shame and injustice of it all. I gave Mr Hummerstone the note Mr Parry had given me for him, sealed in an envelope, and after reading it he tapped me twice on the head with the cane and said, 'Don't get caught doing it again.'

We learned Ar Hyd y Nos—All Through the Night—one Wednesday at the Welsh school. The ability of the Welsh people is remarkable; their method of teaching seemed new and different. Certainly, when we learned to sing in Welsh it lent a new meaning to the experience of singing classes. This was something totally enjoyable. We were taught to harmonise, to roll our 'r's, to relish the words, for were they not beautiful? 'Listen now, boys—'Tyner, tyner, sua'r awel . . .' Sometimes, one of the senior Welsh girls, Tilly, sang solo, and sent tingles down our spines with her lovely voice.

Griff Thomas Bach y Saer—Little Griffith Thomas the carpenter —and Billy Ifanc—young Billy—his son had their workshop right on the village street, suspended on a flint base, at right angles to the other buildings. It had a corrugated iron roof blanketed by prolific ivy creepers, but the timbers were firm, and when I saw the shed thirty years later it was still standing, and the ivy was even more prolific. During cold and wet play periods a few of us preferred to call in on Griff Thomas, and in the company of this man we learned about wood, the feel and the smell of it.

'See this now, boys? This is oak. There's lovely, isn't it? Take a sniff. Eh? Like no other wood, is oak. What we call tight grain, see? And straight as a die. And this one by here, this one is a lovely wood, too. Elm. Funny stuff, but beautifully grained. Big branches can fall off an elm, you know, so don't stand under one in windy weather. We use it for the planking in carts, because it will put up with any amount of wet, and it will last for a hundred years.'

He and his son Billy, who also seemed old to us (although probably only in his twenties) wore blue bib and braces, never anything else; it was their uniform. And sometimes Mr Griffiths wore bicycle clips too, although we never saw him on a bike. They were consummate craftsmen, working with wooden-handled tools that had already been used a lifetime, and their shed was full of the rich smell of woods, for the floor was spongy with layers of shavings and cuts-off. We were allowed to pick up the smaller bits, to carve our aeroplanes and boats. (The aeroplanes were Hurricanes and Spitfires, but we also made a special one with a fat body and double wings with struts, and floats. It could never have flown, but it was fun to make.) We watched in awe as Mr Thomas planed the rim of an oak coffin, the plane sighing over the wood as if lamenting the body it was about to enclose. Everything he and Billy did looked easy. They not only made coffins for the district—which meant at least once a week—but they also lined them and put on brass fittings, so that when they left the shed they looked too good for their purpose. He and Billy made gates, fences, doors, window frames, garden frames, axe handles and all sorts of handles. And they made cart wheels, things of marvellous symmetry and complexity.

'Now then, boys, this is what we call a dished wheel. It goes in from the rim to the hub like a dish, see? When a cart is loaded, the weight makes the wheels splay out, so if the spokes were straight-on, they wouldn't last very long, would they? But, if we make them go into the hub at the same angle that the wheel splays out, well, now then, the spokes are straight up, and they can carry the load without straining, see? When you boys are older you will understand more about carts, and what I have told you will make sense.' But, of course, he was wrong, for the cart went out, and car came in, and all that wonderful skill was to be lost forever.

'What's wrong with Bloss, Mr Jenkins?' I asked. 'She smells like lawn mowings.'

Mr Jenkins came out of Bloss's stable, where she had been left for the last two days.

'She's got grass fever, I think, Dick bach,' he said, looking concerned. 'The vet will be coming soon and then we shall see.'

The veterinary surgeon came, and he and Mr Jenkins and Mr Lewis the bailiff disappeared inside. I tried to climb up to peer through the iron bars of the window but failed, so I hung around in misery.

Bloss was put down with an humane killer, her body dragged out and dumped into a trailer and taken away for burning, and I was desolate. Back in our kitchen, I leaned on the wide white window sill and sobbed, pushing the palms of my hands hard against my eyes to keep the tears in. The grief at losing Bloss was hard to bear. David and Eric and Log and Malc withdrew to the table and sat in embarrassment at my display. I crept up to my bedroom after a while, head bent so that the maids would not see my stained and grubby face, and with my John Bull pen, price five shillings and sixpence, I wrote in my best handwriting,

29

To Bloss,
My favourite horse.
Whose death was through the cause
Of that wretched grass fever,
And I'm afraid I'll have to leave her.

Futile, infantile words with which to grope to express my grief, but I felt better for having written them. Now and then the image of Bloss's carcass being heaved on to the trailer brought a fresh sob, but time healed the hurt. I never forgot the feel of that great black horse, though, and none of the others ever took her place in my affections.

It was some time between summer and autumn of that first year that Lois entered our lives. Lois was the headmaster's only child, older than us by two or three years, a large girl, pretty in the way that large people are pretty, with dark hair and dark eyes and red cheeks. Moreover, she played the accordion with considerable skill. With the coming of Lois, life in our playroom changed. Somehow, we had to accommodate this older and wiser woman.

It was Lois's special skill with the accordion that was probably the chief reason for our forming The Ffynone Gang, that unique party of six which was to transform all previous concepts of entertainment and lend a new meaning to that word. We wore pierrot costumes to perform in, while Lois wore a kind of 'Swiss Miss' skirt and blouse. I wrote a play called *The Bragger* which formed the main part of our tortuous, one hour show, and by chance the leading role fell into my lap, although everyone was a star.

The show began with an introductory song as the curtains drew back:

'Ffynone Gang is so jolly fine,
As you all will see-ee in ti-ime.'

The rest of the song is lost on me. Lois's accordion swelled and drowned our puny voices, and the audiences loved it, clapping before we got into our first line, which was me telling the most

30

outrageously unfunny jokes. However, polite applause followed this too, and when everyone had settled down, we put on 'The Bragger.'

The recollection of the production, directed with patience by the headmaster, brings beads of perspiration to my brow even now, for it must have made all intelligent listeners cringe in the seats of the dusty halls of those villages we visited. We were hunters in a strange and fearful country, lost for the moment in a large cave lit by a solitary candle that cast grotesque shadows on the upturned table that was our cave. Somehow, we rescued Lois from headhunters, at great risk to our lives, and it all ended with another song and the great noise of the accordion, and again the marvellous audiences never failed to applaud. Then there was a collection of songs, many made popular by the war. 'Roll out the Barrel,' 'The White Clifs of Dover,' 'We'll Hang out the Washing,' 'This Old Man,' and many others long forgotten, and everyone sang merrily, making it all worth while. And when 'Mae Hen Wlad Fy Nhadau' was sung, the evening was given a finale far, far greater than our efforts deserved.

One of the concessions to modern farming at Ffynone was the dark green Fordson Diesel tractor, driven by the one-time Englishman Jack Stilwell, he of the thick glasses and large wife and host of noisy children. Jack seemed to be father of the tractor too, for he doted on it, and a blissful expression softened his rugged face as it chugged, blue-smoking across the wide, shadowed fields. It had an iron seat burnished to a fine sheen by Jack's corduroys.

During the corn harvest, when we had the second half of our summer holiday, the old tractor chugged through the long, hot days without respite, pulling a Massey Harris Reaper Binder. Then the air vibrated to the sound of the tractor and the incredible cacophony of clacking, whirring, whistling, slapping of the binder as its windmill-like arms stretched against the sky then curled into the corn to push it into the gnashing teeth of the cutter. Up went the severed corn into a chute, to disappear under a rubber flap. All sorts of noises emanated from the

31

pulsating interior, then out popped a neatly trussed sheaf of corn, bound with the 'corden binder,' picked up by evil-looking prongs and dumped out the opposite side. When the twine broke—which was quite often—bits of savaged corn flew out of the machine from every hole, and there would be mild panic, and Jack would add further lustre to his seat as he stopped the tractor and spun round and, with a choice mixture of vituperative Welsh and English, set to to find the broken ends.

We revelled in the harvesting of the corn. Our principal task was stooking—forming little pyramids of four sheaves in rows behind the tractor, so that they all leaned into each other, and dried very quickly in the summer heat. Even greater fun was the loading of the sheaves into the waggons, when Bloss Number Two and Dandy, Ginger and Bowler crunched over the stalks with their great feathered feet, stopping automatically at the low command of 'Whoa', leaning forward for a few paces to 'tch, tch.' The men pitchforked the sheaves into the waggons, where a farmhand stacked them according to custom so that they made a balanced load, the centre hollowed out for him to move around in. When fully loaded, the waggon made its creaking, swaying way over the yellow field and back to the farm, two or three of us stretched out in the hollow crown watching the pitchfork gyrate gently, and the farmhand sitting on the outside shaft singing a hymn in low, chapel voice. There was a beauty in the natural simplicity of it all.

At lunch times the maids brought out great hampers on a gambo, and laid out on a cloth a vast array of bulging ham sandwiches, tomatoes, plates of patted butter, cottage loaves broken into crisp chunks for men's hands, and an urn of sweet, steaming tea. We all stopped and sat to eat in the shade of a waggon. Nose-bags were fitted over the horses' heads, then with raging hunger and thirst and a sense of utter contentment we set to, and everybody was untouched by the war in that other world. After the meal the men, replete, would settle themselves comfortably for a doze, or a smoke, and we chewed cornstalks and told jokes, and offered the horses a bucket of water each after removing their nose-bags.

It was not all sunshine and wonderment, however. As the summer tailed off into autumn, we spent Saturday mornings wrapped in sacks to keep out the rain and the cold as we loaded mangel wurzels into the muddied gambos, and conversation was bad-tempered. We nearly broke our backs potato picking, heaving wicker baskets along the tumbled soil to the collecting points, our clogs thick with mud. It was labour to which we were unaccustomed, and which we found hard, but as we grew older and tougher in the following years, it became a little easier, and we understood how the old men seemed never to falter. It was all a matter of setting a smooth pace, unhurried, economic, so that energy was not wasted unnecessarily. But this all came with experience.

Autumn drifted into winter, and the fields became dull and lifeless. The animals stood in sheltered corners, our clogs rang stridently on the road to school, and we wore mittens and blew into our fingers. The fire in our Reading Room was stoked with great frequency by Mrs Thomas, who flitted in and out swiftly, smiling an apology each time and giving a little wave if Mr Hummerstone was not looking.

Christmas came; grey, dry, arctic, vibrant with promise. At school we occupied ourselves with making decorations— endless chains of coloured paper stuck with flour and water, and designing Christmas cards and calendars. It was an intensely happy time, our first Christmas from home, full of expectancy. We said 'Nadolig Llawen' to everyone—'Happy Christmas!' When the skies were particularly grey the roads became very white, and we waited for the snow to come so that we would be marooned in the mansion, unable to attend school, perhaps for weeks and weeks. When Old Mr George of Cilgwyn came charioteering up the lane in his milk float, rattling and thundering over the hard bumps, scarf flying behind him like a drogue and hat brim flattened against the crown, there was no cloud of dust. Tough as he was, the cold turned his nose blue and his eyes watered, and he would laugh and say, 'There's cold, isn't it, bois?' And we knew winter was upon us.

The mansion was festooned with decorations. A large fir tree filled the hall, twinkling with a hundred stars, loaded with presents in bright paper tied with silver cord.

On Christmas Eve we made our excited way to the great lounge, where we had never been before, and we sang carols in front of Daniel Daniels, Esq., J.P. and Mrs Daniels, and Mrs

33

Bickerton-Edwards, who regarded us from their deep chairs with smiling affection. The following day I recall that we ran to and fro through the halls in tumultous excitement, showing off the presents that had been hidden from us for this very day by all the grown-ups concerned, even though we saw Twm y Post delivering them. Mrs Hawkins kept them well-hidden from our prying eyes, and the maids would not say who had received a parcel. It did not concern us that Father Christmas would come down a chimney—that was kid's stuff.

At teatime we cleaned up and marched along to the great lounge again, for here it was all going to happen. The tree was placed in the lounge, and we sat crosslegged around it; the maids put their arms around our shoulders and patted our heads and showered us with soft little kisses like snowflakes. We played party games, and every single person joined in, especially the Major. Soon the room was fragrant with a blue mist of cigar smoke. It seemed that all the men smoked, and all the women drank. Then came presents time, and the honour of handing them out fell to Mr Dunne, a task which he undertook with his usual dignity, reeking of wine, and a benign smile on his little grey face.

The long span of years has not diminished the sensation of pleasure experienced at receiving, among the inevitable sweets and chocolate, an autograph book from Mr and Mrs Hawkins and Lois, and a diary from Mrs Bickerton-Edwards. We all received these two presents, but in addition Mrs Hawkins had taken the trouble to invent a small rhyme and insert it in each of our autograph books. Mine carried the two lines, 'The pigeon's egg which wouldn't hatch—it only made a dirty patch.' This marked for posterity one particular incident when I carefully laid under my pillow an egg retrieved from the spinney, only to squash it beyond all hope of hatching when I eased myself off the bed by leaning on the pillow with my elbow.

It was the diary which fascinated me throughout the evening, all next day, and for more than thirty years afterwards. A Charles Letts Diary, in blue leatherette, 1941. It contained an incredible amount of utterly useless but interesting information, liberally illustrated with diagrams.

34

Aeroplanes aerobatics. Boat Races, Oxford and Cambridge. Careers. Countries of the World. Daily wants. Dates, interesting. Equivalents French Verbs, German Strong Verbs. Logarithms. Nautical Measures. Phrases, Foreign. Records of our Modern World. Trigonometrical Formulae.

I read the pages avidly, with growing excitement. This was something new, pocketable, an easy reference to interesting titbits. I would try to pigeon-hole every scrap of information, become a font of knowledge, Walker the Brains. I absorbed the facts that a 2oz letter costs 1½d, Southern Rhodesia had a population of 1,581,000 the Beano cost 2d weekly, Meccano Magazine 6d monthly, and the record for the mile was 4 min, 6¾ seconds. I could not wait until January 1st to insert my first entry, so in the memorandum part I wrote, 'December 26th, Our Play The Bragger at Ffynone. Presents off the tree. On 27th at the Welsh School Party. Santa Claus was Mr Edwards Pentre. Had a Jigsaw.'

The Christmas Week passed in an orgy of sweet things. Parties were exchanged. There was no snow, only a lowering grey sky that threatened with icy blast the coming winter. An ugly incident marred the final day of our holiday, for which I was responsible.

We were trudging up to the farm, wrapped up in our Lease-Lend sweaters and blue raincoats, clogs sounding empty of flesh on the iron-hard ground, when we saw a broom waving a mock surrender at us from behind the cowshed wall. Without really thinking, I bent down and prised a stone out of the ground, and flung it at the broom quite twenty yards distant. I shouted something about Indians. There was a sharp snick of sound—I had hit the broom. It disappeared, and we cheered. Our cheers were abruptly cut short as a dead-white face blotched by a great puddle of blood on the right side, rose in sight above the wall, and a strained voice cried out, 'That was a bloody stupid thing to do, boys!' It was Gwilym Lewis the cowman, second only in our affections to Mr Jenkins. We were aghast at the hurt, the bloodied face, the anguish in Mr Lewis's voice. We turned and fled in panic in all directions, ending up back at our playroom in dribs and drabs, where we discussed the incident in hushed voices, guilty as pariahs.

35

Within an hour it was common knowledge throughout the mansion, as we knew it would be. I dreaded facing Mr Hawkins, but he was very kind about it, seeing my distress and quite aware that the incident was unintentional. He took me up to the bailiff's house where Mr Lewis sat with a bandage round his head, covering one eye. With Mr Hawkins at my back, I mumbled my heartfelt apologies, on the verge of tears. Mr Lewis instantly forgot the whole thing, splendid person that he was, and I cried in relief as he pulled my cap over my eyes. But his scar over an eyebrow was to serve as a permanent reminder to me of the folly of throwing stones at people.

And so 1940 drew to a close, cold, dry and grey. None of us had shed a tear for maternal comfort, nor had there been wistful talk of home. We were too well looked after, too busy and too happy to worry about events in the world beyond Frenni Fawr, the mountain four miles away. Our parents were finding things more difficult. My mother said she waited three weeks for a torch to see over the golf links on her way home, and another two weeks for two batteries, and one of those was a dud, and during that time she twisted her ankle four times.

A few names linger from the period. Churchill, Lord Haw-Haw and Tommy Handley and Vera Lynn—but Strang the Terrible and Desperate Dan were more interesting to us.

We carved Spitfires and Blenheims and Fairey Battles from scraps of wood, and we had mock air battles with them down the village street, in defiance of the real Nazi attacks on Holland and France and Norway at this time. We sang 'Rule Britannia' on the way to school, marching as we sang. At times, the grown-ups looked quite glum, speaking with unease of the Jerries being only twenty-one miles from the English Coast, or three hundred and sixty miles from Capel Newydd.

January 1st.
Snow. Dai's Birthday (11). Letter from Mum. 2/6 P.O.
New horse came to farm. West wind, 6-7 mph.

36

At school, I was Wind Recorder. I picked up my wind rag first thing and tripped out to our field and held out the rag at arm's length, facing the wind. There were degrees of fluttering; a limp wave was just about 2-5 mph, and as the flutter increased so the windspeed went up by fives. Crude, totally unreliable, but essential to our weather chart which we religiously maintained. I had always been a child of the weather, being happiest on fine, windless days, dejected to the point of being a bore when it rained, and bad-tempered when the wind howled and moaned through the trees.

We nearly had a real tragedy on the farm one Saturday morning. It was an over-bright day, the ground dazzling with thick, crunchy frost. Our feet froze in our clogs, and we skipped about the farm to try and kindle some life in them, and blew into our gloves, so that the breath vapourised in clouds about us. We ended up in one of the hay annexes to the stables, huddled in a nest, thumping each other. Then Eric disappeared from sight. He tipped backwards against the wall, his legs went up, he gasped, and was gone. Even in the split second that it took for him to disappear we were fortunate enough to grasp one leg by the ankle and clog. We held on to each other, the hay, the wall and the roof joists, we grabbed anything and yelled. Somehow, we managed to drag Eric up from the dark cleft in which he hung, choking from the dust and hay chaff, unable to breathe. He emerged, blackened and inarticulate crying and coughing, and we lay back with him across our laps, suddenly hot, no longer frigid with cold. The incident frightened us, for we knew that Eric could easily have suffocated to death. I don't think we ever went into that shed again, but kept to the haggards where there was daylight on all sides.

On the way to school one snow-laden morning we came across Mr Dunne along the drive. Not in person, but his image was unmistakable in the deep snow where he had fallen from his old bike, all spread out and a little dent where his hat had left his head. We found this hilarious, and laughed all the way to the school. Later, we heard that Mr Dunne was quite proud of his snowgraph, and had brought the maids to look at it, and it stayed there for many days, before gradually disappearing.

Sunday, 12th.
Maurice Newman's Birthday. Went to church.
Received 1d for collection from Mrs Hawkins. Mickey made a
mess in our playroom. Took medicine. Went down the dingle at
night at 7 o'clock.

The Sunday Event—a walk down through the Ffynone forest
with the headmaster and Mrs Hawkins and, sometimes, Lois.
She seemed to be forever doing homework so she did not often
join us. Wellies on, blue raincoats, knitted woollen gloves.
Scramble along the corridor and up the five steps and into the
courtyard. Jog about impatiently in a five-boy huddle until Mr
and Mrs Hawkins were ready to go, emerging arm in arm,
headmaster with his walking stick third-legging the wet-leaved
ground.

We skip and trot, side-step and jump, puddles cleared in one
bound, cart tracks straddled, special leaves squashed, branches
swung on, dead stalks snapped and thrown as spears, trees
circumnavigated, headmaster and Mrs Hawkins hidden from,
then pounced upon, while they strode purposefully on down
the dingle and we all became enclosed by the tall and dripping,
listening, leafless trees. Now and again we zoom in on Mr
Hawkins, align ourselves, pause for breath, walk sensibly for
ten seconds. Unofficial school.

'Why does it always rain harder just before it stops, sir?'

'Sir, why are tree barks different?'

'Why don't snakes blink, sir?'

'Why have hares got bigger ears than rabbits, sir?'

We bombard the headmaster with such questions like air-to-
air missiles, then zoom off again without waiting for answers.

The Dingle Walk in winter never bored us. We were like
puppies being taken out by their master. The air down there
always seemed to pluck the lungs with cold fingers, the trees
had a watchful look, and the ground made little, marsh-like
plops as if gasses had come to the surface. We would arrive at
the waterfall, the pride of Ffynone, a thirty feet high cascade
that plunged down into the frothy black water below which
narrowed into a crystal bright stream as it wound its way to the
lake. We could jump across this stream on to a tiny island of

pebbly soil and this became one of our tests for admission into our 'Just William Gang.' You were allowed three attempts. Further along, the stream became six feet wide, and here you had to clear it with a leaping pole. The noise of the waterfall drowned most other sounds, and we had to shout to each other, but when Mr and Mrs Hawkins came with us, we remained reasonably quiet, for they liked to stand on the bank for a while and admire the water.

The lake was a wide stretch of brooding, dark water. Dead trees were like grey fingers nudging the water's edge, reaching up in despair for the sky; reeds shivered as water rats and water fowl moved amongst them. Rings appeared by magic as fish prodded the surface. We were wary of the lake, even when it glistened in sunlight, for it was not a friendly place. The water had a dead look about it. When we leaned over the stone parapet of the lodge, we sometimes saw great eels sliding along the weed-slimed wall below waterlevel. Sometimes, too, we saw Daniel Daniels, Esq. hunched in his little square boat, casting flies. Awed, we would watch him in silence in case we frightened off the fish and made him angry. Silence lay over the lake like an invisible blanket, creating a kind of sad peace, a graveyard peace, and we would emerge from our loud cavorting in the woods to be subdued by the sight of the water. It was as if we were entering some holy place where dire punishment was meted out to little boys in wellies and blue raincoats who made a noise.

Sometime during that first winter, Eric's younger sister died of diptheria. There seemed to be a minor epidemic of it over in St Dogmael's. That evening, in our playroom, we strove to play a hard game of piggy-back with Eric, to keep his mind off the tragedy and also to keep the presence of death from our world of make-believe. We succeeded for a while, and a game was in full swing, and we had Eric and his horse penned in a corner behind the settee, when suddenly he crouched with his face to the wall and began to cry. Silently at first, then with a choking kind of snort, and finally with great, convulsive sobs, and we stood and looked at each other bleakly, feeling a collective sadness for him. The rest of the evening was morbid. We were unused to tragedies. They spoiled all the fun.

Jan 16th. Snow. Snowball fight at school. Fell over three times.
Chauffeur's daugher (Ffynone) got married to a sub-lieutenant.
Had for supper a piece of wedding cake, trifle, and 2 cakes.

I recall the chauffeur's daughter as a slim, fair young lady
who strode the fields all around, catching moles. She wore a
flowing coat of moleskins that was faintly scented, and at her
waist she wore a wire on which were strung half-a-dozen or
more moletraps, evil looking things that crushed the moles to
death when sprung. We escorted her on her rounds for a few
mornings and evenings. She could tell at a glance which traps
in the little earthmounds had been sprung, for the arms would
be together—when freshly set, the arms were apart. When she
first handed us a dead mole we thought it rather fun, and we
handled the fat little limp bodies with interest. But before very
long the indifference of this efficient huntress to the suffering
of moles killed by the trap method paled on us. We felt for the
moles, and left her to her hunting, for we had better things to
do.

We did not see the wedding, but we saw the arrival of all the
guests, and we stared in admiration at her husband in uniform,
and fantasized about his submarine exploits, knowing him to
be a sub-lieutenant.

Jan 18th. Heavy snow. Played snowballs. Making model with
my Trix. Beaza had a little calf. Had a bath. The plug doesn't
work right.
Jan 22nd. Had a haircut up Crymmych. Wrote letter to Mum.
Bought some chocolate. 2d. Played Whist with Mr Hawkins.

Mr Hawkins had one of the few cars in the area, a snug little
green Austin Seven, CKR 724. Somehow, we all crammed into
it on the wet days, when walking to school was a real trial, and
we took it in turns to sit in the front. On very cold mornings hot
water had to be poured into the radiator, then we took it in
turns to crank the engine with the ignition off, so that the oil
circulated. Then, with the choke fully out, and all of us standing clear, Mr Hawkins started the engine. If everything had
been correctly seen to, the engine fired first time. It was a drill
that we thoroughly enjoyed. Cars, in those early war days,

were a real luxury. Only a few of the more wealthy farmers had them, or could get the petrol coupons to run them. Here, at Ffynone, we had the estate car, a beautiful Morris with a long bonnet that Mr Davis the chauffeur would let no one touch, and the headmaster's car. We were highly privileged.

Our winter evenings were never dull. In our playroom we had half-a-dozen chairs, a settee, two tables, an electric fire that made our hands tingle when it was not being used because the wiring was faulty, and a shiny lino floor on which to slide in our stockinged feet. The room was about thirty feet long by fifteen, large enough and cluttered enough to afford us plenty of scope for hide-and-seek and other, more strenuous games. We had our Trix and Meccano sets, jigsaw puzzles, pastels, paints, crayons, snakes-and-ladders, Ludo, draughts, and cards. But best of all were the invitations to play Whist with Mr and Mrs Hawkins and Lois in their cosy, open-hearthed, wingback-furnitured room across the passage. There was a rota of sorts which ensured that we all had a game. We discussed our games afterwards with real pleasure, especially if we had won, as this was like winning a gold medal. Whist was the ideal game for us, requiring just the right amount of thought before playing a card. Bridge was mentioned now and again, but I think Mr Hawkins weighed up its complexities against our ability, and came down in favour of retaining Whist. After each evening of cards, the non-players would be invited in, and we'd all have hot cup of cocoa and biscuits before being packed off to bed.

Thurdsay evenings were devoted to letter writing, even if we had already written. There was no evading it.

Lois spent evenings with us in our playroom when she was not doing her homework. She was not a tomboy, but she had a great sense of fun and her presence rarely restricted our games. It was nicer squeezing into a corner with Lois during Blind Man's Bluff than with one of the other boys, for she tended rather to envelop one with her softness—it was like being crushed with a big feather pillow. Because of the environment in which she spent all her days, she Knew About Things, and she was already in her early teens. Sometimes she would enter our playroom and sit down, and eye us all in a mysterious fashion, one by one, without saying a word, a little smile on her face. She knew we did not know what she knew. At times we messed about around her, workers round a queen bee, showing off, and she seemed to enjoy being the centre of attraction. One night Mrs Hawkins caught Malcolm under Lois's bed, but Malcolm assured us the next morning that it was all innocent fun; he'd wanted to play draughts with her in peace and quiet without us lot hanging over his shoulders. Mrs Hawkins did not seem too upset at the sight of Malcolm's feet sticking out from under the bed and certainly there was no animosity at breakfast next morning. She may well have thought that if Malcolm had more evil intentions towards Lois, he would have left them until much later, when we were all asleep. Lois did drift into our bedroom one night, and ask David and me if we would like to See Her, and opened the top of her nightdress for us to do just that. It was rather nice and unexpected, and we collapsed in giggling embarrassment as she drifted out of our room, all of us flushed.

We made camps out of the furniture, and assault courses, testing the quality of the chairs to an undreamed-of standard. There were times when Mr Hawkins stormed in and forbade us to make another sound, we could be heard all over the mansion and God knows what Daniel Daniels thought of us. We always slid about in the playroom, because shoes were forbidden. The maids tidied up our chaos every morning, we untidied it every evening. Sometimes Mrs Bickerton-Edwards paid us a surprise visit, and the silence as she stood in the doorway was deafening as she viewed the uses to which the furniture was being put.

Jan 25th, Saturday. Went up to the farm. Saw Beaza's little calf. Lost my knife. Carting hay. Jumped about 15 feet from the haggard. Played Whist with Mr Hawkins in the evening.

My fifteen feet jump was in fact a long, slow slither, taken after nearly an hour of dares from my friends. It seemed a very brave thing to do. When finally I could not drag my body back from the brink, there was a second when I fell free before thumping into the hay below and bouncing high, unhurt and exhilarated. The jump then became a regular event, and we incorporated it into our Tests.

42

Sunday, Feb 9th. Went to church with Mrs Bicky-Eddy. Mr and Mrs Hawkins went to Pendine. We had meals with the maids. We borrowed the gramaphone from Mrs Bicky-Eddy, and records.

The gramophone was of rich-smelling black leather, with bright chrome head and green base, and a handle with overwind safeguard, and it played the 78s magnificently. We stretched out on the settee and on the floor, and listened to Vera Lynn songs, for she was the rage at the time. 'We'll Meet Again,' 'The White Cliffs of Dover.' There were Nelson Eddy and Jeanette MacDonald, Anne Zeigler and Webster Booth, a host of Victor Sylvester strict tempo records to which we danced with impossible movements. It was a rather nice way of spending the hours. And on Sundays we had our little cups of Virol before going to bed enriched and fortified.

Sunday mornings were devoted to church, without fail, unless we were ill, which was an extremely rare occurrence, and always viewed with suspicion by Mr and Mrs Hawkins. On fine mornings we left the mansion early to walk the three miles to church, but in inclement weather our friendly Austin would take us in two journeys. A half-mile from the church was the other great house of Pentre, where we would hang around whistling and waiting for the Edwards girls and their brother Norman to appear, for their father was head gardener and the large family occupied Pentre Lodge. We were all in the choir together. When the girls appeared my heart would thump at the sight of Dorothy, and we would exchange sly smiles that the others pretended not to notice.

Carregwen, our church—its name means White Rock— nestled in the shade of yews with dark, secret shadows, and its graveyard is full. All the services were in English, even though the congregation was mostly Welsh. Our vicar was very English, as was his wife, and their son was a bit of a sop to whom we felt protective when he impinged himself on our company. Dorothy's father was choir leader, an always-smiling, sweet tenor-voiced little man whom everyone loved, for he seemed not to have a mean streak in him.

We saw the same faces every Sunday. They sang with un-restrained energy, proud of their good voices. In the front pew

43

sat Mrs Catcheside and her children, a clan apart. Londoners; it was said that she was a Prima Donna. I remember her for her splendid presence, for she was large of limb and bosom, and handsome, and she wore a fox stole whose little beady eyes glinted at you when she took a deep breath. When she sang, little shivers would run up and down my back, her glorious voice filling the church, echoing along the high beamed roof and through the pillars, trailing off beautifully—perhaps reluctantly—just a fraction later than the rest of us. And I would wish that it could go on forever.

As the sermon dragged on, the boys eyed the girls and the girls eyed the boys, and notes were passed by hot little hands under surplices. Once the vicar, becoming unusually theatrical, held out his arms, intoning, 'He looked towards Sodom. He made his journey to Sodom. He dwelt in Sodom!' We were enthralled by his outburst, and for weeks we relished the word Sodom, using it like a swear word and feeling very manly because of it.

> *Monday, Feb 10th. Made a bow and arrow. Malcolm met his Mum at night time. Eric had a letter.*
> *Thursday, Feb 13th. Put 1/- in National Savings. Took my truck to school. Cyril gave me a peashooter. Dai caught a little rabbit. Swore in the New Ffynone Gang. Broke my peashooter.*
> *Monday, Feb 17th. Found another nest of rabbits, four bigger ones. I am in charge of three small ones. Saw a big rat up the farm. Bought chocolate up the village. 2d worth.*

As a child, one of my less endearing traits was a cunningly concealed meanness at its best—or worst—whenever I bought myself a bar of chocolate. I would share chocolate with no one. A twopenny bar of chocolate would last me all the way back to Ffynone, without my having to dawdle. And I recall this particular evening, a promise of further rain in the low, scudding clouds, and the wind moaning through the cables that sagged from post to post like empty washing lines. It was about five o'clock, a couple of hours before our supper. The people at Brynawel Stores had given me the usual friendly greeting, 'Hello, Dick bach, how are you, then?'

44

Passing the chapel, my mouth already bulging with the first mouthful of chocolate, I paused. It was a nice old chapel, clean and square and wide-windowed. I clopped up the small path in my clogs and sat on the stump of an old yew tree, drawing my macintosh about my knees. By now it was almost dark, and cold, and the wind moaned higher. And in that quickening period before rain begins to fall, I was overcome by a sense of profound loneliness. Not an aloneness, for that never occurred in such a close, rural community. This was a sadness deeper than anything I had ever experienced before, and so personal that the tears filled my eyes and I began to cry, the bar of chocolate clenched in my hand. I suspect this mood touches us all at times during the passing of our years; an inexplicable sensation sent, perhaps, by taunting spirits from an unfriendly world. This was the first time I had experienced such intense solitude, and I have not forgotten it. I wandered back to Ffynone dejected, the wind at my back. The rain did not come, and I was able to finish eating my chocolate without having to offer one little square to anyone.

Feb 21st. Went to the station to meet Beagley. Waited two hours. Air Raid at Swansea, saw fires and lights out of our bedroom window. Map drawing at school.

Donald Beagley was a latecomer from Hythe. We knew him for always being late for roll call, always panting up as we mustered, always with a ready excuse for being late. And here he was, late again. Late-again Beagley. Ten years old, lean and dark-skinned with wavy, black hair and bright, mischievous eyes. (The girls were to sigh when they came to know him.) The headmaster settled him into the village shop with the Thomases, where Mr Thomas called him a Gipsy Boy, and we all laughed (except Donald). It was after we had left him that there was time to wonder at the orange glow in the sky that emanated from the devastation of Swansea, and we spoke in hushed voices as we looked out over the dark fields from the snug safety of our bedrooms. There really was a war on, and here it was, not three hundred and sixty miles distant, but only sixty. And right at this very moment people were getting killed.

45

Saturday, Feb 22. Went to Abercych with Fatty and Bing.
Fatty got his clogs. Bing came to tea.

Donald was immediately called Bing, I think because he used
to drone 'boo-boo-boo-boom' in imitation of Bing Crosby. We
took him to our mansion, walking to the village to pick him up.
We walked him down to Abercych, then to Ffynone, and back
to the village when it was dark. Altogether we must have
covered six miles, in the slow pace that children have when
they are occupied with swinging from branches, throwing
stones at targets—foxgloves, thistles, telegraph posts—and
seeing how far they can spit. In retrospect it seems that we
never had to hurry anywhere, were never bound by time limits,
and it was certainly safe to walk about in the dark without fear
of assault.

We had Marble Tournaments. Marbles were sold at the
village shop in all sizes and the most exquisite colours. Some
were nobler than others, larger, and they were worth winning.
Others were smaller and plainer, dwarfs, and were kept as a
last resort so that they wouldn't get chipped, because once a
small chipped one began to roll it could go anywhere except on
course. We sometimes had a quick game on the way to school,
kneeling and sighting and flicking them with the thumb and
scurrying to pick up both marbles after that marvellous sound
they made when they struck one another. We huddled over
them when they were close together, making sure there was no
cheating, and carried them proudly in little bags with draw-
strings, like Jews with their money bags. During the play
periods at school we had exchange sessions, mulling over each
other's spoils, testing for weight, two small ones for a big one
(for a big one rolled further in a straight line than a smaller
one). There were so few vehicles around that it was safe to
occupy the middle of the road if necessary, and this sometimes
resulted in meeting players coming the other way. All in all,
playing marbles was a good way to pass the time of day, and we
developed great skill with our thumb flicking.

Newchapel—Capel Newydd—straddled both sides of the
main road which ran from Abercych to Boncath. It took twelve
seconds to pass through from one end to the other at thirty
miles an hour in headmaster's Austin. There were no back

46

streets nor alleys, just a couple of private paths leading into small fields, a lane to Cilgwyn Farm and down to the Cwm, one going up to meet the top road, and one becoming a drive between the lodge gates of Cilwendeg Mansion. From the crossroads three hundred yards above the village (there was a gentle slope downwards towards Boncath), the four roads ran to Llechryd, Ffynone, Abercych and Boncath. The first house on the left, in a group of three, belonged to Mr Thomas Stiff Leg, the genial carpenter for Ffynone Estate and caretaker of our school room next door. A Great War wound had resulted in his losing a kneecap, so when he mounted his tall black bike, he rode with his leg stretched out straight, like an oar, balancing him as he strained with his one stirruped leg in the other pedal and waved and called 'Bore Da' to everyone he passed. Next door to our school room lived the District Nurse, a lovely cheerful lady who tended our cuts and bruises and peeling ears. Then Cilgwyn Lane, our own very special playground, a haunt of fort-riddled hedges and deep grass and marble-stopping white dust, its honey-beed air rent apart with the cries of our battles. On the other side was the dry stone wall surrounding the rock cottage of quiet Mr Williams, whose son was aircrew and away fighting for us all and who had already ditched into the Atlantic in his bomber. Next door was the Top Shop, now on the point of closure, and next to this Mr Evans y Beic. He was in his seventies, tall and heavy in his blue serge and bicycle clips, red-faced and humourless, an ex-cycling champion (so it was said). He did not regard us with much love, but I was to find a smiling elf deep within him under his tight-buttoned waistcoat. Twenty yards of hedge on the top of another dry-stone wall brought you to Brynawel Stores, the busy village shop of Twm Llewellyn Thomas, champion gardener. Another hundred yards of stone wall led to the Lodge gates of Cilwendeg Mansion; and that was the extent of the village street. Opposite Brynawel Stores, on a bank and surrounded by foxgloves, were two adjoining cottages. The first belonged to the Wooldridges. Mrs Wooldridge was a dark, handsome woman with quick, clog-clacking walk and shrill voice, whose husband was an ex-miner suffering from 'the Dust' and whose son, Alun, shared as little affection for us as we for him. Dai Rees y Gof—the village blacksmith—occupied the cottage next

47

door. He was the blacksmith of all people, the definitive strong man who had mastered the intricacies of metal gates and wheel tyres by a sublime gift for his craft. He was short and straight-backed, broad and square-faced handsome, a man's man, rich voiced. His arms were white and massively muscled. He wore well-worn blue serge, the crutch of his trousers very low so that his legs looked shorter than they were, and the belt was pulled in well below his stomach, giving him a narrow-hipped appearance, and his white shirts were collarless. His forge was dark, silenced by a hundred years of smoke and grime and dust. A long shiny handle stuck out from the huge forge bellows, and we would pump this handle when the fire was required, our feet leaving the ground on the up stroke and we wriggled like eels to get it down again, two of us endeavouring to do the work of Dai Rees's left arm.

Farmhorses from far and wide came to the forge. Some were nervous, most were docile, and one or two were rogues. Dai y Gof knew all of them, spoke and cajoled and cursed as appropriate, but was never cruel to them. We liked the smell of the hot shoe placed on the hoof, the yellow smoke that billowed out with a hiss, and the sound of his rasp. Many of our play periods were spent in the forge, but he seemed not to mind our being under his feet and plying him with questions when he was busy.

A rough, ankle-twisting lane that led to the top road separated the forge from the Ffynone Arms, a long stone building with a cattle byre under one wing, a sloping forecourt of stone flagging, and the village pump set on a large slate outside its front door. The two Evans boys and their parents worked hard at their small-holding as well as the Arms. We got on well with the family; once, Mr Evans showed us his Naval Officer's uniform in his wardrobe, and it always remained a mystery to us why he never went back to sea. We knew nothing of Defer-rment, of course. At right angles to the Arms was the Home Guard Hut, out of bounds to everyone, a secret place full of lists containing the names of spies in our area (so we were told by an unsmiling Mr Evans who said we'd be shot if we told anyone).

Then came the Chapel. It stood square and solid in front of tha trim lawn. It was said that when, in 1763, the Reverend

Howell Davies passed through Capel Newydd on horseback, he noted the lack of a place of worship, so he said, 'I shall throw my whip, and where it lands, so shall a chapel be built,' and so it was.

A tiny, overgrown lane that trickled in a bed of nettles separated the Chapel grounds from our other favourite venue, the carpenter's shed. There followed a line of three small houses, the lane to the Welsh school, a fine detached house where the Lockyers lived, and then you were out of the village and heading towards the crossroads. That was the extent of our world; a sprinkling of cottages, a few lanes, endless foxgloves and nettles, countless hiding places, and people who always had something to say to us. It was an exciting little world from which we derived immense pleasure. Not that every day was idyllic for there were times when we felt forgotten and disliked, when tempers flared and there was trouble, when we cursed the endless ritual of church and school, when we arrived at school soaked, or freezing, after the long walk in foul weather from the mansion. But in general my diaries are a record of delight in trivial things, of pleasure and fun.

Sunday, Feb 23rd. Bing came to tea, afterwards went down the dingle. Wrote my story.

My 'story' was to be the ultimate in detective stories. It began well, with a headless corpse lying across a hedge, to which painful position it had fallen from the open bedroom window of a lovely old house and a detective was called, who inspected the corpse and said with grim finality, 'This person is dead, and he has been murdered.' Somehow, it never recovered from the damning observation, and petered out.

Tuesday, Feb 25th. Saw some soldiers come by in lorries. We all gave them three cheers (West Kents). Gave girl at the nurse's a note from one of the soldiers.
Thursday, Feb 27th, Halfday holiday. Acted our play at Boncath WMCA, turned out well. Cyril went to Haverfordwest to see about his eyes.

Cyril was the odd man out in our class, due almost entirely to his extremely poor eyesight. His eyes stared hugely from

49

behind steel-rimmed spectacles, both in slightly different directions. He always looked trussed up in too small a jacket and trousers, which may to some extent have had an adverse affect on his athletic prowess. He had an outstanding gift for drawing cows, which he must have studied meticulously—he was billeted two miles out on a smallholding. His cows had mighty udders, and they were beautifully muscled. We all liked Cyril. When we played hide and seek we tended to move when it was his turn to find us, so that we could be detected a little easier. Otherwise he could walk right by us. His father was an Army officer, who once paid us a visit and we were very impressed by his shiny badge and Captain's insignia.

Saturday, March 1st. Parcel and 2/- from Mum. Went to the Pictures and saw Pinocchio and Goat Tales.

The cinema was in Cardigan, seven miles away. With about four shillings in our pockets we panted up to the village and waited outside Brynawel Stores for the old bus to appear, which it always managed to do, no matter what the weather was like. Within seconds of its eleven o'clock scheduled time of arrival, it would come chugging round the Lodge corner from Boncath, but we knew by its own particular sounds when it was coming before it came into view. The bus ride was part of the adventure, for we invariably stood in the aisle at the back so that the grown-ups could have the seats, and with any luck the Edwards girls would board and join us at Pentre, and there would be huge smiles all round, then the Lawless girls a bit further on, then a couple of our chums from outlying farms, so that eventually the bus bulged with a crowd of yelling, laughing boys showing off shamelessly to girls and passengers.

At Cardigan the first priority was shopping. Money was no problem, for most of us still had three shilling and two pence to spend. We bought pencils and rubbers, a packet of envelopes and a writing pad, a little green frog with a bottom of a tar-like substance which held a spring for about ten seconds before releasing the frog with an energetic leap in the air; a lead farm animal, plasticine, a Fairey Battle or a Wellington bomber, a cardboard glider, a small jigsaw puzzle, caps for our pistols and rubber for our catapults, a penknife, The Beano or The

Adventure, Tip-Top and Jingles, The Dandy with Strang the Terrible. And always a bar of chocolate. Then a dash down to the bus station where you could buy a hot roll with butter, before racing to the cinema.

The cinema was a low, wooden building. The queue stretched all round it, a milling huddle of schoolchildren interspersed with an occasional and disapproving adult. Entrance Fee, 2d children, 6d adults. I always despaired at the size of the queue, certain that we would never get in, but not once were we ever left out. I think it may have been a kind of expanding cinema, magically absorbing any amount of children. Once inside, there was bedlam, children calling to each other, the dust rising in clouds from the bare boards, the rushing to and from the toilet—if only in order to pass a girl, and the girls shrieking because the boys barged past them. The music grated and shrilled continuously from the speakers, adding to the din. Then, when the lights dimmed, the place was transformed, due to the awesome presence of a stern Great War veteran with faded ribbons on his old blue suit. He would march around the auditorium and with stentorian cry and stick in the hand soon have everyone in his seat. He smashed the backs of the seats with his stick so that the dust coughed out in clouds, and at last the adults could enjoy the film. Anymore trouble and the offender was grabbed and hustled out amid muted cheers.

After the pictures there was a mad rush to the bus station, where the fat lady sold hot buttered rolls, and then a lazy wait around for the bus. The journey back was always much quieter; we were weary, scruffy, and usually penniless. Then there was the plod back to Ffynone in the dark, a tiring journey now, and we seldom met anyone, and there would be the slightly rebellious feeling against church tomorrow.

Thursday, March 6th. Frank came back to school. Finished painting my picture at school. Threshing at the farm. Saw hounds and two huntsmen up the village. Ron had a letter.
Thursday, March 13th. 1/7 for Arithmetic. Finished my painting at school. Saw Elizabeth.

Elizabeth was a true Romany. She looked almost Indian as she came swinging down the village street during our lunch hour, hand on the halter of the leading skewball, long printed dress

51

almost touching the ground, her matted black hair hanging in tangled ropes down her back. There were two caravans in Elizabeth's family, four horses, a number of lurchers, some chickens, a couple of dark, fat women and three or four swarthy, bright-eyed men. They usually camped above the village in what we called the Gipsy Wood, and after school we ran up to their site to help Elizabeth gather faggots, stroke the dogs and horses, and smell the cooking of their food. Elizabeth spoke in a strange accent which we found difficult to understand, and made us laugh. We liked her for her strangeness, the imagined mystery of her, and we gaped at her wisdom and knowledge of things, for she must have been sixteen or seventeen. We often saw the men emerge from the woods loaded with potatoes or beet or turnips which they had doubtless borrowed from the clamps in the fields; and they would make their meal over bright fires, talking their strange tongue, seeming not to mind our inquisitive presence. We sometimes went back after our own tea and sat under a caravan and stroked the dogs, which appeared to like strangers, and once I had a steaming cup of tea handed to me by one of the women, wordlessly but with a smile, and I drank it with my arm round the neck of one of the dogs. Not once however, were we allowed even to sit on the steps of their caravans, nor to peer inside. Whatever possessions they owned were screened from the prying eyes of all strangers, and this set the level of our acquaintance with the gipsy people. They were mysterious, tolerant, not too clean by our own standards, and secretive. But in their own way they were kind to us.

Saturday, March 15th. Went to Cardigan for a haircut. Took Bowler to smithy and back again. Went to Pendine. Saw wrecked German plane, took a piece, and a piece of a British plane.

There seemed to be one barber to serve the needs of all Cardigan and the surrounding area. He was large and never moved because he had two artifical legs, so he perched on one of the bowls. He had three or four assistants. There were always at least twenty people waiting, standing and sitting. Once inside, if only to take stock of the queue, the command 'Aros!'—'Wait!' compelled one to do just that, trapped, small against the tall adults. The barbers snicked and combed, pulled

52

and chopped and brushed and sprayed with practised speed, and the customers always said 'Good' to the proffered mirror. They stood up from the chairs all brilliantined and shorn, the towel whisked off their necks in conjuror's fashion, producing by magic their new looks, and they were dismissed to the call of 'Next!' And there you were, towel thrust round your neck and under your chin and the scissors already to work. No man-to-man politeness now, no 'How would you like it?' All the boys received the same haircut, and no mirror—who would dare to have criticised, anyway? And no Brilliantine. That was for the men. We had something wet enough to plaster the hair down for a couple of hours, and that was 6d. 'Next!'

Thursday, March 20th. Went down the Dingle to get some daffs. Got a sword and spear. Went gardening. Fed the horses up the farm after tea.
Friday, March 21st. Did drawing daffodils at school. Went up the farm after tea. Went to the mole traps after tea. Did the Weather Chart. Ron had a telephone call.
Thursday, March 27th. Went up the farm after tea. Saw Ginger being washed in the duck pond. We were innoculated at the Session Room.

I usually experienced a mixed sensation of trepidation and excitement when the doctor or the dentist arrived in their large white vans. The vehicles themselves were impressively large, very important-looking. The equipment was carried into our schoolroom, and one at a time we would be led behind a screen and stripped to the waist if it was to be the doctor's examination or, in the case of the dentist, seated in the chair that was designed to inspire fear into every child. When the examinations were over, and the medical team gone, there was a sense of anti-climax. No one had anything wrong with them. We all, at one time or another, had fillings and teeth removed and I remember the dreadful pain of an extraction when coming out of the gas-induced sleep. Everybody, including the dentist, was surprised at the noise I made.

Friday, March 28th. We had a half holiday from school. Mr Hawkins went to Narbeth. Eric ill in bed. Dai had a parcel. Soldiers came to look at the mansion.

53

We were in the playroom when the soldiers came, officers in smart uniforms and gleaming belts, polished men, very English. They smiled at us when Mrs Bickerton-Edwards opened the door and exhibited us to them. Afterwards we heard whispers of a coming change in the not-too-distant future, when Ffynone would become a convalescent centre for the war-wounded. But that was not to come for a while, so there was no need for us to worry about changes and we could continue living in our cossetted world. I can remember the complete lack of concern at being ousted from the mansion and being deposited in the great big world outside.

April 4th. Fine weather. Went up the farm and set my traps. Ron had a parcel. after tea, David and I went down Gwyn's place and played with Nicholas. Dandy went to the blacksmith. Saw the Hythe Major.
April 17th. Daisy had two calves. The sow had 8 piglets. Cleaned out cowsheds up the farm. I killed one mouse. Played tracking after tea.

This was our first spring in Wales, and it was refreshingly new, for we live in an area of miniature valleys. One could look down on the wooded valleys contained by the steep hills and see all the new, vibrant colours, and they were beautiful beyond words. The lanes narrowed with the abundance of new growth spreading out along them. We went tracking through the brilliant undergrowth, stalking one another with spear in hand, searching for clues, pretending to be the Last of the Mohicans, or bandits, or cowboys, whatever took our fancy. When we carried our bows and arrows we were Robin Hood and His Gang, or Just William and *His* Gang.

Ron had a fist fight with Muriel Mawr—Big Muriel—in the village street, right outside the schoolroom. I cannot remember how it began, but it was probably a shoulder shove as the Welsh children and we came into contact as they walked through our numbers on the way to their school. Suddenly there was a scurry of bodies, a parting, and Ron was squaring up to Muriel, both of them enclosed by the ring we formed. Muriel was quite five inches taller than Ron, and she clenched her teeth and stumped towards him and lashed out, just like one of us, but with much more venom and strength. Ron had adopted the classic pose of the Noble Art, body turned, left out, right guarding his square little chin, and he ducked and moved to one side and prodded out his left. He didn't actually hit Muriel, but she was surprised that he was still there, in dispute. And there he stood, a stalwart and diminutive figure, our Ron, in clogs and jumper and short trousers, evading Muriel's massive swipes with an ease that caused us to whoop with surprise and delight, as his left continued to prod out, then his right. Neither opponent was touched. It was as if each was protected by a cushion of air that prevented every blow from coming into contact. They approached and parted, prodded and lashed out, danced to the right and to the left, never taking their eyes off one another, looking fearsome and grim; but there was no damage. After a couple of minutes, for that is all it could have lasted Muriel kicked out with a great clogged foot, missed, hissed 'I'll see you later, boyo!' turned, and strode off with arms swinging in anger, followed by a silent retinue of supporters. There was little doubt that our Ron had won a moral victory, and we were immensely proud of him. In retrospect it seems astonishing that no adults came out to see what it was all about. Muriel did not come back to see our Ron, and the event passed without a simmering vengeance.

Monday, April 21st. Went up to the farm. Saw pig cut open by butchers. Went to the village letter box on Megan's bike. Mr Hawkins birthday.

We had not witnessed a pig killing until this day. Starting out for school we passed through the farm and along the lane towards the Ffynone road. We saw and heard a pig being hustled by a couple of men in one of the adjoining tiny fields, and since we did not recognise the men we stopped by the gate to see what was happening. The pig had a rope tied to each foreleg, braced stiff with resistance, and a man held on grimly to each rope. Then another big man emerged from the hedge, as if he had been hiding from the activity; in his hand a large knife. He knelt in front of the squealing pig, which by now probably sensed the inevitable pain about to be inflicted on it, and without preamble he stuck the knife into the pig's throat, ripping it open with a rapid, flashing movement, and got to his feet and walked away. The two men released their ropes to watch the pig, gurgling in agony, sway in a tottering, frantic circle on the grass, blood pouring in a fearful torrent from its livid throat. We jumped off the gate and fled in horror, aghast at the blood and squealing and the indifference of the men.

Mrs Bickerton-Edwards had asked us if we would be willing to help her weed the front terrace, and we said yes because we could not say no. The terrace was forbidden territory at the front; we lived in the domestic's side wing. We lined up and listened to instructions. We would have a fork each—an eating fork—and a small knife, and we were to prise out all the dandelions and clover between the granite slabs of the terrace. To make things easy, Mr Dunne would provide us with boiling water to pour down the cracks to loosen all the roots, so it would be fun, wouldn't it?

We set to, squatting in the way that children do, and Mr Dunne emerged, immaculate as always, white towel over his arm, a silver jug held erect, and he stooped grandly to begin his pouring job, for all the world like our vicar offering the wine at communion. I think that our knives were also silver—they were certainly not old yellow-handled things which are used for odd jobs in most homes. The evenings were idyllic, and the ground warm and we sang songs like 'Old Man River' and 'This Old Man' and some of the Welsh ones that we knew, while Mr Dunne poured away and we snicked and heaved. Now and again Mrs Bickerton-Edwards and Mrs Daniels came out to help us, beaming with plasure, casting elegant shadows as they walked to and fro. We continued this pleasant pastime for nearly a week, for the terrace was large, and when we had finished it looked rather grand.

Sunday, April 27th. Went to church. Saw the Bishop of St David's. Went for a walk after dinner. I was told I was going down the Bottom Shop (billet). Cold, cloudy, bright intervals. Tuesday, April 29th. Almost completed my rabbit hutch. Found a mouse trap. Got the cane from Mrs Bigg.

The Hummerstones had left. We were sad at their going, for Mrs Hummerstone had spoilt us, and Mr Hummerstone, though strict, had a sense of fun that endeared him to us. I was not to see them both again for forty-one years. In their place had arrived Mrs Bigg, wife of Mr Bigg, who taught much further away and was known to be a hard man. By all accounts, we were to be in for it. She was a lean lady with a thin brown face and long thin nose, and hair done up in a bun, and she wore exceedingly high-quality Scottish wool skirts and stockings and jackets in winter and summer, so she looked as though she suffered from the cold. She had a beautiful Scots accent, soft and slow, for she came 'from the Isles'. She was very firm, intensely fair, without favourites in our turbulent class, and she played the piano rather well, but not as well as Mr Hawkins. We learned many Scottish songs, among them 'It's a Far Coolin that is callin' me away', and she looked sad, pensive when we droned 'Speed Bonnie Boat'. We sang in a semi-circle around her, and she would call out the beat with her lean brown hands describing brackets, and when she sat at the piano we made faces at her in the cruel, thoughtless way that children do these things. There was no vindictiveness; we rather liked her, and respected her cane arm very much, for she had a wiry strength. She got as much out of us in singing lessons as Mr Parry did in the Welsh school. She made no bones about what was required of us.

'You, Cyril! Stop that stupid noise or go and sit down if ye dinna feel ye can cope. And you, Dick. If you don't wipe that idiot look off your face I'll do it for you.'

When she resorted to the cane, it hurt. 'Why does a nice looking boy like you act like a fool, so?' she wanted to know of me. Hand out-stretched, my eyes averted, swish! A blazing, burning hurt, not always across the fingers but sometimes across the wrist. Defiant stride back to one's desk, fighting back tears of pain and self pity and humiliation. Sitting, squeezing one's burning hands tightly under arm-pits and devising all kinds of torture for that poor harassed lady who was trying to instil some kind of education into us. Caning always had the desired effect—it made one think before doing the same stupid thing again. It did none of us any harm. On the contrary, we became rather less childish because of it. We

57

thought she was a tough old bird, our Mrs Bigg. Old? I doubt that she was forty five.

Wednesday, April 30th. Wrote to Anunt Mary. Saw Mr Jenkins and Emerest (Emrys) race Dandy and Bowler to the fields. Bought two bars of chocolate.
Thursday, May 1st. Had drawing at school. Had fifty lines to do for Mrs Bigg. Went out to play after tea.
Thursday, May 8th. Drew wild flowers at school. Got a little rabbit off Ken and kept it in my hutch. Named it Trixie. I killed two mice up the farm Trixie has a broken foot. Not bad, though.
Saturday, May 10th. Doug Stacey's birthday. Went to Cardigan and bought a new suit. Caught a large rat in my trap.

We set our traps cunningly all over the farm in order to reduce the frightening number of rats and in this we had the blessing of all the farmworkers, as long as we did not endanger the lives of the other creatures. The rat I caught this Saturday morning was monstrous, more the size of a young badger. In its struggles it had left a leg in the jaws of my trap, and then dragged itself round the corner of the shed. We followed the blood trail, found it huddled under a slate, and promptly dispatched it with Indian war-whoops and clogs. We had all the compassion imaginable for the creatures on the farm, disliking the sight of mice caught in our traps even though that was the only object for setting them. But we despised rats. It was the way they slithered like long lumps of wet clay from corner to corner, making a rustling sound. They also frightened us, and because of this we were cruelly disposed towards them. Our mousetraps were little oblong boxes with a trapdoor operated by an elastic band, and a piece of bread or cowcake left at the back, on a platform linked to the elastic band. When the mouse attacked the food, the lid sprung closed, and we had a live mouse. Sometimes, though, they managed to execute themselves on our wicked 8in traps, because we set them so finely as the risk of losing a finger when putting them down and covering them with dust. We only cheered when a rat was caught. (Once, I caught a rabbit in mine, where I had set it on a rat-run on one of the walls. The poor creature had suffered terribly, and we asked the bailiff to dispatch it, and the incident filled us with sorrow. Rabbits were our friends, our pets.) When the thresher came to the farm there was a frenzied chasing of rats by farmworkers and the dogs and us, with wild slashing about with sticks, but remarkably few were caught.

Mr Hawkins drove us to Cardigan in the Austin Ten, and while the others were left to occupy themselves, I was taken to an outfitter for a new suit, my first long trousers and waist coat.

I well remember the outfitter, tape around neck, thin glasses perched on the brink of his nose, hands clasped prayer-like, saying to Mr Hawkins, 'Now, sir, I think he will come off the peg', and I had a mental picture of myself spread-eagled on the wall at the back of his cloth-smelling shop, all nicely fitted out as I hung there.

My suit of blue serge, with faint white stripes, and shiny-backed waistcoat, fitted admirably. I did not feel my youth slipping away as my legs became encased in these baggy, turn-upped trousers, for I already knew that they would be worn only on Sundays and Special days. My mother must have paid the five pounds for my suit, because I certainly didn't, and I had no more coupons left. It was going to have to last a long time—
years.

Monday, May 12th. Beated the carpets for Mrs Hawkins. After tea we had a good game of soldiers. Got the cane off Mrs Bigg. Pentre boys moved into their new billets.
Wednesday, May 14th. Helped to carry Eric's things to the Cwm. Had a haircut off Mr Jenkins. Late for school because I forgot my gasmask. The little rabbits all gone.

Eric's new billet was a stone cottage deep down in the woods that we knew so well, and he was eager to move there, for he knew that the inhabitants and he were going to get along well. I carried a Trix case for him, and boys' magazines, and boxes of plasticine and other essential things, and he carried his suit-case; we left everything at the solid, clean old cottage with Welsh greetings ringing in our ears and went to have our last haircut from Mr Jenkins.

Mr Jenkins was, I am certain, sad at our going from the mansion. He laid a bowl over my head. Any hair that stuck out was prey to his shears, and he said in an attempt at jocularity, 'I ought to keep these curls, Dick bach, and make a pillow.' He kept stirring our memories with 'Do you remember . . . ?' There was an air of departure about the whole evening we spent with him. He told us that Megan, who with Betty and Myfanwy spoiled us completely, was nearly in tears, because the mansion would never be the same again. We believed him; Megan was his only daughter. She was very pretty. Eric and I could only say 'Yes' and 'no' and pretend that we didn't mind leaving all that much, really.

> *Thursday, May 15th. After tea, chased a rabbit in the Kennels Field. Mickey the cat got shut in our playroom and it-er-stinks now. Dai found a shilling.*
> *Saturday, May 17th. We moved from Ffynone in the evening. I went down Brynawel Stores (Bottom shop). Slept with Donald.*

It is strange how we remember all our lives a galaxy of irrelevant images and details, yet forget important events, strive to remember a face or a name or a deed. I cannot remember leaving Ffynone. There must have been a busy few hours of packing, and there were certainly goodbyes to all the lovely people of the mansion. Mrs Bickerton-Edwards in particular had taken a real interest in our doings. There had been one Sunday in every month when Mr Dunne beckoned us one at a time from the playroom and led us with great dignity along the corridors and up the winding staircase to the sun-filled room upstairs where Mrs Bickerton-Edwards sat regally in an ornate chair. I recall the meetings with her, sitting opposite her with my hands under my bottom so that she wouldn't see how I chewed my nails, and shyly answered her questions about my health and how I was getting on at school. And yet I cannot remember saying goodbye to this splendid lady, nor to her clan. I remember helping to beat the massive carpets strung out on lines, when we beat them with bamboo canes and the dust rose into the bright air like smoke against the sun. I remember Mr Jenkins, the horse smell of his corduroys, the brass buttons of his waistcoat, and his gaiters. But I cannot remember leaving Ffynone. It is almost as if nature has eradicated the event from memory to spare me any regrets, so that the transition we were about to undergo would be painless. The mansion had been a home beyond expectations, idyllic. Other mansions in the area had housed boys, but they had not the elegance, the pedigree, the graciousness of Ffynone. We were blissfully unaware of how privileged we had been to have lived at Ffynone, for the Daniel Daniels clan were already a dying breed of a very special people. We were leaving behind forever a life-style which we had taken for granted, but I am sure that Mr and Mrs Hawkins must have been more appreciative of it, and much more saddened at departing. Only the passing of time, the changing standards, have made Ffynone an endearing memory.

Part II
Closer to Earth

Brynawel Stores nestled in thick-walled detachment in a small hollow at the end of the village, the last building before the Lodge further down. One front window was blacked out with Typhoo Tea and Reckitt's Blue and Bisto sun-bleached posters, the other window displaying a magnificent fern in a large brown pot. A path led down to the low front door, and this in turn opened to the left front room which was the shop, our Botton Shop. A room with a hundred scents and smells and odours, of fresh bread and sprouts, potatoes and cabbages and boiled ham, chocolate and Suttons Seeds, of beetroot and Dubbin and polish, and of boiled sweets and onions and sweetpeas. A real shop, a shop of another age, warm and dark. There was a shiny counter and wooden till without a tillroll, packets hanging from beams, stamps under bottles, and an orderly chaos of boxes and cartons and jars. Scissors hung from hooks, invoices from nails, calendars from drawing pins. There were bits of notepaper all over the place. There were clog laces in strands, raffia in hanks, and balls of string on pegs. You could buy almost anything at Brynawel Stores, late into the night too, for as long as the light was on it was open for business, with no policeman to read out the Shop Act. It was a shop for which normal hours and emergency hours were indefinable.

The living room at the back of the shop was tiny, about ten feet long by six feet wide. A step led one down into the equally long and narrow kitchen, and out to the large shed at the end, which was really an extension of the house. A kitchen range easily disposed of all waste and, as in all kitchens, was a vision of gleaming green metal and polished brass, and it whined with heat, emitting little gasps. A Welsh settle snuggled up to the stove on one side, while the dining table with four chairs occupied the other, and there was a sideboard crammed with newspapers and coupon pads and a bakelite radio. We had electric light, for electric supplies had come to Capel Newydd many years ago, but all hot water had to be boiled on a paraffin stove as there was no hot water system from the kitchen range. Consequently a large kettle softly whistled to itself all day and every day perched on the paraffin stove. The Front Room—

the other room—was hardly used during the week, only for passing through to go upstairs. It was spotlessly clean, and had a large table with a prickly green cover on which lay a Bible, closed and forbidding. Upstairs were two large bedrooms at the front, and our bedroom with a sloping roof, and a boxroom full of cardboard boxes. I was going to love this old place.

Mr and Mrs Twm Llewellyn were in their mid-fifties when I arrived, although I thought they were very old, because they had grey hair. Twm Llewellyn was a 'character,' still remembered. He was a champion gardener with a showcase of thrice-won trophies in the front room to prove it. He was a good-looking man, small and stout with middle age. He leaned a little to one side, favouring his good leg; the other one was false, made of leather that squeaked when he walked. He had an enormous sense of fun, and shook in silent laughter instead of guffawing, so that other people found this infectious and laughed with him, too. Mrs Thomas was also small, with hair tightly drawn into a bun, and she too was nice-looking, neat, quick of movement, but more thoughtful than Twm Llewellyn. There were two daughters, Eirlys the elder by about six years and then in her early twenties, and Megan. Eirlys was like her mother, Megan like her father, Eirlys dark-haired and slim, Megan fair and sturdy. She was a close friend of Lois.

Sunday, May 18th. Went to Chapel. Didn't like it very much. Mrs Thomas showed me a lot of photographs.

There was the pre-chapel ritual to be subjected to before Donald and I left the house, and that was a hard, swift brush down by Eirlys. We'd stand in the shed, and she used a Mason Pearson wire brush on our suits, almost brushing us into the ground in her enthusiasm to remove the most minute hairs. And she said the same thing everytime, 'It's the worst of these dark suits, they show all the hairs,' and her brush drove smartly along our shoulders and down our backs.

The chapel was tall-windowed, with sky-reflecting plain glass like blue steel sheets, and varnished door with great brass knocker that was never knocked, with narrow path between the two trim lawns and a dead stump where the old yew used to cast its deep dark shadow. On one side the caretaker's house, pebble-dashed and black-windowed with careful curtains. And on the other side, the long, low red brick annexe, ugly and modern beside the holy white of the chapel, where we had tea parties and junior chapel every Tuesday evening.

Inside was waxed and polished silence, wood and paint cleansed of all sin. The glass of the lanterns gleaming liquid, brass shimmering at the small, plain pulpit and the small, plain altar, for there was no ostentation here. The empty family boxes held open their doors, waiting for the families to rustle quietly in. And silence in the gallery above, reserved for other chapel-goers who came once or twice a year to sing at the Pwnc, a gathering not to be missed, when our chapel would overflow.

At seven o'clock in the evening seventy voices would tremble in contralto and soprano, tenor and bass, some gifted, other only partly so, but all rendering the evening beautiful and haunting with their music. Chapel has begun. Canu pob un— everybody sing.

Morning chapel never had the fire of the evening service, and afternoon Sunday-school even less. I now had to get used to the Sunday routine of chapel—or our own church—in the morning, and chapel in the afternoon and evening, and on Tuesday evenings when the slender and darkly handsome Mair George taught us. The long hours of freedom that we had experienced at Ffynone were a thing to be remembered with longing. Now, we were in our best suits all day, so walks had to be kept in a low profile; tidily, as we were told.

My first attendance at chapel was with all the family. There was no preacher that morning, so the service lasted barely an hour. Afternoon Sunday school was quite fun, as the Welsh boys and Donald and I got on well together, and most of the talking had now to be in English. A preacher was coming in the evening, and I was warned by Donald that the nice times were over—I'd be bored stiff. The service would last two hours. Next Sunday, the preacher would come in the morning. Chapel always alternated like this, and the only way to avoid the preacher was when he came in the mornings, as we could then go to Carregwen. We had the choice, of course, of going to our own church every Sunday, or attending Chapel. Generally, especially when the weather was good, we preferred to walk the three miles to church.

67

Preparation for that first evening service in chapel was quite a revelation. Mrs Thomas brought out the Bible, the Testament Newydd.

'You must learn a verse for Mr Rees-Davies, Dick bach,' she said. 'Now then, we'll learn an easy one, just three words. 'Wait—ah, here it is. Now, say this after me. A'r Iesu a wylodd.'

I repeated it. Easy.

'And Jesus wept,' said Mrs Thomas. 'That is the shortest verse in the Bible. And you can say it first time. There's good, now then!'

I had pleased her, and myself. Already I could quote a piece of the Bible, take my place with pride in the queue between the pews, and when my turn came, announce loud and clear that Jesus wept. Donald also had his piece to learn.

The service began quietly enough, with the preacher entering the pulpit and uttering a quiet prayer. Then we sang and there were more prayers, a little louder, I thought. Another hymn, then a settling down in the pews and boxes, a few coughs, a deal of rustling and creaking of tight shoes, a wink from Mr Thomas, and the preacher began, with a verse from the Testament Newydd. He spoke in Welsh for more than an hour, gradually warming to his subject, getting taller and bigger, his arms reaching up and out, down and round, embracing the lantern, the heavens and all hell, and his voice rose higher, stronger. At times he paused, and a dramatic silence settled over the rapt congregation, all eyes turned to him, all souls wishing to be purged. Then the splendid voice would resume, on a low key, swelling into full cry. Now and again Mr Thomas, who seemed to absorb this all without much trouble, quietly produced boiled sweets from a pocket, the faint rustle of sticky paper bringing a sharp glance of rebuke from Mrs Thomas, and they were passed round with exaggerated stealth, only Mrs Thomas shaking her head in refusal. Fancy eating sweets when the Reverend Rees-Davies was preaching after coming all this way. Whatever next? Sometimes we had peppermints. By the time the preaching was over, Donald and I were ready for anything. And in all truth, I think the hymn immediately after a long preaching session was always the best, as if everyone were releasing tension, exploding.

When my turn came to speak my verse, I uttered it faultlessly. 'Now then, fachgen, why did Jesus weep?' I was asked by the preacher. And I was stunned for an answer, for Mrs Thomas had not given me one.

Monday, May 19th. After breakfast Donald and I brought Bess in from the field. Played down the wood in the evening. Got a wet foot.

Bess, a small Welsh hunter, was already eighteen years old, slightly sagging along her back, but sweet-tempered and unbelievably wise, or cunning, or both. She trotted up to the gate only if she could see a bowl of corn being held out, and it was no use pretending that there was corn in the bowl. You had to shake it so that she could hear it. Sometimes, as we were about to put the halter around her neck, she'd decide to have a game, and veer off down the field, giving us a merry chase between the nettles and thistles. We took turns in riding her back with a halter. She pulled Twm Llewellyn's trap, a handsome vehicle with spidery wheels and slender shafts, dark green with fine black lines emphasising the shape of the side panels, and so light that Donald and I could push it with ease.

There were four rounds to do every week, calling on small holdings far and wide to deliver goods and collect eggs. Once hitched up and the trap loaded up, Bess was pointed in the right direction—guided to one of four ways out of the village— and left to her own good judgement. She knew every stone, every slope, every hazard, she knew where to step wide on the dangerous hills, which gates to enter, and who would give her a piece of bread or a pat or a handful of corn. Her skill was faultless. Twm Llewellyn sat most of the time just smoking his pipe, and singing to himself, occasionally talking to Bess. She had retained a vast store of sounds and sights in her head. In the winter evenings, when she was tucked snugly in her stable adjoining the shop, she neighed on hearing Twm Llewellyn's artificial leg creaking as he walked to the outside toilet in the garden, and when he came down the village street after Sunday evening chapel. Donald and I never gained the affection she had for him; she tolerated us.

Thursday, May 22nd. I gave sixpence to an old poor man for singing. Had three cuts of the cane off Mr Bigg. Rained hard. After breakfast I brought Bess back from the field. After tea I played Draughts with Tom Bach in his house. I won 5-1.

Tom Bach was the father of the lady who looked after the chapel and lived in the adjoining house, the Chapel House. He was known as Twm Bach y Capel—Little Tom of the Chapel. He was tiny, barely my size. His daughter was tiny, and she had a tiny baby, too. Her husband was away in the war, so I felt quite a man when Mrs Thomas asked me to pop up to the Chapel House now and then, and give poor little Mr Tom Lewis a game to pass away the evening. We played by the light of a brass oil lamp, little Tom in his brown suit, neat as a tailor's dummy, puffing at a tiny pipe as he leaned over the draught board, and his tiny daughter and granddaughter curled up against the open fire, watching us, smiling at every move. She was breast-feeding the baby, and I strained my eyes to catch a glimpse of her tiny white breast, peering through the fingers of my head-propping hand. The evening sped by, the oil lamp hissed quietly, the fire murmured and sparked, and tiny Mrs Phillips cooed and smiled and the baby sucked and gurgled, and Tom Bach floated in a cloud of aromatic pipe smoke. When the clock struck nine it was time to quit, the game was called a draw if unfinished, the draughts packed away, the accumulator radio switched on for the news. 'Nos da, Dick, a diolch yn fawr,' and I would be ushered out, to trot back to Brynawel, barely a hundred yards down the road.

The Nine-o'clock News was a very serious event for the adults. Twm Llewellyn would settle himself down by the range, feed tobacco into his pipe, waiting with a rapt look on his face, and we knew better than to interrupt. Alvar Liddell broadcast the good news and the bad, but in 1942 there seemed to be precious good news. And to Donald and me it was all unreal. It seemed stupid, grown-ups killing each other like this. We said that Churchill should take on Hitler in single combat, that Churchill would win because Hitler had only been a corporal and so couldn't have been much good anyway. While Twm Llewellyn smoked, and Mrs Thomas and Eirlys and Megan knitted, we painted or crayoned. When the news ended, it was a hot cup of cocoa, a wash, then 'Nos da, boys.' If we were still awake at ten o'clock, reading in bed, we would hear the news again, in Welsh. 'Dyma'r Newyddion yn Gymraeg, a Hywel Davies yn ei ddarllen.' 'This is the news in Welsh, read by Hywel   Davies.'

Saturday, May 24th. Went to Cardigan with Mr Thomas and Eric and Mrs Davis in the afternoon. I went to the Pictures with Mrs Davis and Eric. They were not very good. I bought a wooden spoon in the market. Cost 6d. H.M.S. Hood sunk. MANY DROWNED.

When we heard this news on that evening, we were sitting cosily in the back room, the table littered with green, yellow and pink food coupons which we were cutting up and storing in their relevant piles. There was stunned silence. Twm Llewellyn had a look of horror on his face, and they all looked at each other. Mrs Thomas laid her hands on her lap, like two dead doves. 'There's terrible.' They looked empty then as if the war was lost, and Donald and I felt the tragedy touch us too. It was not all one big game, not really.

Friday, May 30th. After tea, worked in the garden, did good work. Donald had a letter. Eric went to Newcastle Emlyn, didn't come to school.

There was no doubt that our garden was the best one in all the valleys. It was not very large, about thirty yards by twenty, with a couple of Beauty of Bath apple trees in the middle to break the expanse, and two rose arches to lend the path a little dignity and style. The soil heaved and writhed with the healthiest, largest worms I had ever seen. It was black soil, made extra special with seventeen years of manure from Bess's stable at the top end, and with rabbit's manure from the cauldron by the shed. Everything sown or planted grew effortlessly to immense proportions, losing nothing in quality. All around the air was scented with mint. From the third day of my arrival I became totally involved with the working of this garden. Here, things were done properly; the crops stood to attention in straight lines, peasticks were all cut level, straight

71

ash poles used for the runner beans, the holes in the watering can kept clear, the trees pruned for shape, the mint bushes kept small and compact, the paths hoed as soon as weeds appeared, and the soil itself kept absolutely free of weeds all the time, and digging done properly because 'no matter where you went in life, if you could dig well you would be alright.'

As Donald and I toiled at our jobs, with Twm Llewellyn creaking up and down the path keeping an eye on us, Evans y Beic next door would sometimes lean on the dividing hedge and encourage us in a patois of English and Welsh, 'Dammo, these bois is da iown, aren't they, Twm? I said you was very good, bois bach. Keep at it now then, Gwaith—work, bois bach.'

We often worked for a couple of hours most evenings that summer, being rewarded with a bar of chocolate between us, or a sherbet or two. It was a business arrangement to our mutual satisfaction, equivalent to about 2d per hour. We helped Frank with his work if we were free and he was not. At some time in the evenings Frank could be seen sagging under his yoke of two buckets of water, filling up at the pump outside the Arms, and staggering up the lane to the Wooldridge's smallholding. Frank was uncommonly sturdy for his age, so he was given a man's work. We'd take it in turns to carry his yoke to the water trough in their small field, and with our help he would sometimes get away with us down to the bottom spinney or up the crossroads, the Outlaws Wood or the Fern Wood.

The woods were splendid places in which to play, criss-crossed by countless paths, with many small ravines which had to be cleared by leaping pole. We managed to build platforms in some of the trees, with bits of wood nailed into the trunk in order to climb up. In these we pretended to smoke cigarettes, sucking at elderberry stalks. When we went down to the Outlaws Wood, we crossed the field by leaping pole, mole hill to mole-hill. It was a fine test of skill from which we derived enormous fun. We went tracking each other in the Fern Wood, splitting up, running off to the count of a hundred. I think this was our favourite game. It called for a high degree of stealth. I remember sighting Frank's pullover in a fern thicket, and creeping soundlessly up to him and tapping him on the head with my spear. 'Gotcha!'

72

Later on, Double Summer Time gave us all the hours we needed for work and play. As the sun went down the men returned home from the fields tired, dust-black, and we sometimes trudged back to the village with them, equally tired after our long day. In our fourteen waking hours we went to school worked in the garden, and often on one of the farms, or took messages two or three miles away, played, and still there was not enough time to do all we had planned. Boredom was unknown to us.

Tuesday, June 3rd. Went down Cilgwyn. Had tea there. Found a linnet's nest, five eggs. Afterwards, hunted for a lost heffer. nearly trod on a large viper.
Saturday, June 14th. Donald's birthday. Found a nest of baby hedgesparrows. Don and I painted a wheel each of the pony trap. Made a new hutch. So did Don. Don had a letter. Gave a penny to the Red Cross.
Sunday, June 15th. Didn't go to church. Found a nest of six baby rabbits. Went to chapel in the afternoon and evening. Claudia fell off her bike. Sunny weather.

It was a mellow, bird-song evening. Chapel was over, everyone who did not live in the village had slowly departed, but a small group of us remained, spread out on the shop wall; three of us boys, Twm Llewellyn, and Mr Lawless y Llath—the milklorry driver who was father of the three lovely Lawless girls. Talk was of onions and lorries, horses and crops, a slow, wide-ranging conversation between two men who knew that we boys hung on to every word. From the wall we had a clear view up the blacksmith's lane, and in the other directions. It was an evening for looking along streets and lanes, and whittling with penknives.

Mr Lawless squinted up the lane. 'She's coming a bit fast, isn't she?'

We, too, stared, and saw either a woman or a girl hurtling down towards us on a bike. We could hear it thudding and clanging against the pitted and uneven surface of the lane. It was a wild kind of ride.

'Tell you what,' said Mr Lawless, 'I don't reckon she's going to stop.'

73

We watched her approach, skirt billowing in the air, now only about fifty yards away, and there was a simultaneous movement of bodies as we heaved ourselves off the little shop wall and quite involuntarily dived into two groups, leaving a clear passage for the bike. Not so much clear as unimpeded. Then we saw that it was Claudia, the Pentre gamekeeper's daughter. Her face was taut, her arms strained desperately at the handlebars, and she was trying frantically to backpedal. But there was no stopping her assault. Down she came, past the forge, across the street, and into the shop wall. She catapulted with astonishing speed over the handlebars and landed upside down in our best rose bush, displaying white knickers and flailing legs. We collided with each other in our haste to rescue her from her thorny bed, taking care nonetheless to avoid the thorns that had trapped her, and found that miraculously she had escaped with just a few bruises, some scratches, and an enormous sense of humiliation. The bike acquired a new, impractical shape to its front wheel, and the pedals were in poor shape, but nothing that could not be repaired. Considering the perilous circumstances and the impact, the event was not without humour. It made our day.

Thursday, June 19th. Changed my tank for a lorry and two trailers off Roy Humphreys. After tea went down the Cwm to see Eric.

The fields at this time of the year were pocked with rabbits' nests. We knew which ones held young by the bits of fur adhering to the mouths of the holes. There were few nicer experiences than the feel of the warm, cuddly bodies at arm's length down the burrow. We all made rabbit hutches from scrap wood and stocked them with young rabbits, feeding them with young lettuce leaves, little realising that this diet killed them. If they didn't die, they escaped. Only Frank's survived against all odds, losing a tail in the process. All our rabbits were called Lucy or Trixie or Jenny. Wherevr we went there were rabbits; the fields were full of them. The nights were torn apart with their screaming when Jack y Trapper came to the area and laid his gin traps.

74

We secretly called Jack the Trapper, Spanish Jack, because we thought he had the looks of a pirate of the Spanish Main. He was an official rabbit trapper, and covered a very wide area. He had a pony and trap, the latter clinking with its load of traps. He would trap three or four fields at a time, catching fifty to a hundred rabbits, which he sold locally and to the other villages, for they made an excellent pie. (Rabbit pie, cold, was one of our regular dishes.) There were nights when we crept down to the fields and out of compassion released the shrieking rabbits, only to see them run into another trap. It was a distressing business, for there were victims other than rabbits; stoats and weasels, badgers, and numerous birds.

> *Monday, June 23rd. We have been in Wales one year. Lucy got away but got caught again. Trixie died. Don lost one of his rabbits. Eric came up the village to play. We went bush beating.*
> *Saturday, June 28th. My birthday. Don and I went to Aberporth with Mrs Thomas. Had a swim there. Saw a man bathing there with no legs, and walked on his hands. Had dinner and tea there. Enjoyed myself. Had a small present from Lois.*

With the exception of Cardigan's muddy estuary, this was the first time we had seen the sea since our evacuation. I can remember vividly feeling the excitement at the prospect of bathing, a sensation which has never diminished through the years. Perhaps there is, after all, something of the crab in Cancerians. I know we pounded across the sands of Aberporth and splashed whooping into the sea with great war cries. There was no barbed wire, we were free to bathe where we wished. We couldn't actually swim, but we made the motions, and that counted as a swim, and Mrs Thomas had no worries about us drifting away on the tide. I couldn't take my eyes off the legless man, and I was astonished at his agility, for he swung his torso between his arms in order to get along.

A Bofors unit was poised on the cliff overlooking the sands, and during our picnic lunch it fired a few shells which Donald and I saw fleetingly as they sped skywards, although Mrs Thomas said we were imagining things. We explored a few of the cliff paths, stopping at one place to peer over the edge of the cliff. Below us were two lady bathers, one sheltering the other with her body while she removed her wet cotsume. We held our breath, bursting with anticipation. The Bofors gun fired. I looked up and yelled, 'There's another one, Don!' and the woman below us looked up.

'You nasty little sneaks!' one of them screamed, perceiving us hanging over the cliff, but the rest was lost on us. We got up and ran off, laughing like idiots, but sorry that we had missed the performance of a lifetime.

Tuesday, July 1st. After tea played with my soldiers. Trixie died. At school went nettle collecting to get them for medicine for doctors. Had the cane off Mrs Bigg. She cut my thumb.

Nettle collecting was our first contribution to the War Effort. They were required for their drug content, and all schools were to organise parties for their efficient harvesting. We could wear what we liked, as it was regarded as free time from the classroom, so many of us arrived in complicated preventative garb, from sacks to our billetor's old overcoats and in wellies and with thick gloves or mittens. We came armed with sickles and hedgeclippers, secateurs and sheep shears, anything that could cut. The only danger was involuntary amputation. Soon the nettle beds down Cilgwyn lane were devastated, and those of us with leather gloves filled the huge bags we had been given, and they were left at the side of the lane to be picked up and transported the three miles to Pentre, where a large shed had been allocated to us for their drying. I was given the job of Raking Master, because, said Mrs Bigg, it would keep me quiet for an hour everyday. I would be loaned Mr Hawkins' bike.

It was a job that I thoroughly enjoyed. The bike ride was a pleasure itself, for one part of the journey involved a steep little hill with a curve at the bottom, so you could really 'do a Spitfire' on the bike. The shed was large and warm and quiet, semi-dark, raised on pillars ten feet above the ground, so there were steps to mount. I raked the nettles every day after lunch, and each day they made more noise as they became drier, until after a week or so they were all curled up and quite dusty. In this stage they were bagged up and dispatched, and we went down the lanes and demolished other nettle beds. It was a fine way to be helping to fight the Hun. What really surprised us after a few weeks was a cheque that arrived at the school. We were actually *paid* for this enjoyable task. All the nettles had been weighed. We had earned one pound, eighteen shillings and sixpence, which was shared out among the nineteen of us. We were rich! What a war!

On Saturday, July 15th, my freedom was severly curtailed by the arrival of my mother, who was to stay a fortnight at the Ffynone Arms. Other mothers had come down and taken their sons back, because the threat of invasion seemed so remote. I didn't want to go back. There was too much going on here to miss. My mother brought with her my roller skates, which made me unique. I found the village streets very unkind to them however, and barely had a chance to show off in front of my pals and the Welsh children—who had never seen skates before—when to my sorrow I realised that the rims were going to come off.

When my mother arrived, the villagers found their excuses to come into the shop and look her over, and they all said, 'Duw! there's a difference! There's a likeness in the face, mind you— but her hair is black as jet and there's Dick with his so fair.' She was then forty two. To my child's eye she was quite old, and when we went for walks it embarrassed me that we had to go so slowly. But she liked my world very much, and this really surprised me. One fine day she and Megan and Donald and Eirlys and I walked all the way across the fields and up the lanes and through the heather to the summit of Frenni Fawr—no small feat. She walked to church with me, and down to the Ffynone waterfall, and to Abercych and to Pentre and Cilwendeg. We had tea with the headmaster and Mrs Hawkins, and mother was assured that I was average in all subjects, if only just, and after seven days she went back to Hythe, to the war zone, and did not take me with her, and I was free to get my skates out.

Sunday, July 20th. Fine weather. Went to Church in the morning with Mr Hawkins, and chapel in the afternoon and evening. After evening chapel went for a short walk with Mr

77

Muriel and the viper

Thomas. He put my name on a slate up the top school. Saw grasshoppers in chapel.
Tuesday, July 22nd. Fine weather. Went gardening in the afternoon. After tea played with Muriel Reece, Frank and Alun. Muriel Killed an adder.

We were in the Fern Wood, Muriel and Frank and Alun and I. It was a truce period between Alun and me, when we talked quite civilly to each other; at such times I thought him not such a bad chap, all said and done. Muriel suddenly pointed and shouted, 'Look by there!' So we did, and saw a large adder coiled happily and lazily on the warm earth. It appeared to be looking at us. Without a moment's hesitation Muriel jumped on it. Her great knotty legs in their ankle socks and clogs pummelled like pistons, her arms flailed, her skirt swirled, and she yelled and we yelled and the snake didn't have much chance. In seconds it was all over, and Muriel was holding out the snake to us boys, who were less brave, less strong, less manly than she was. In a moment of madness she had shown that she was better than any of us, wiping out in those few frantic seconds any doubts we may have had of her ability to outshine us in courage. Not that I ever doubted her strength—she made light work of a yoke with two buckets of water.

———

It was time for Tests in Geography, Composition, Dictation, Reading, English, Spelling, Writing, Mental Arithmetic, Poetry and History, with a total possible mark of 420. While we hunched over our lined exercise books, hot hands clenching wooden pen with steel nib, village sounds echoed all around us. Sawing and hammering, click-clack of clogs up and down the street, shrill greetings, laughter, hens and cockerels clucking, cows lowing, horses clopping and waggons creaking. I came ninth out of nineteen in the class of 1941, accruing 287 marks, thus stamping my mediocrity on all about me, and it was no use my complaining that I'd have done better had there been Art, which was my best subject. I was in two minds about poetry. I loved the Rudyard Kipling poems, and had learned *If* by heart. Robert Burns' work we all found baffling, but John

Donne was impossible. History I found an absolute bore, simply a catalogue of dates of not very exciting events, and I did not acquire a passion for it until it was too late. However, I got hold of Nada the Lily by Rider Haggard, and that changed my attitude to other histories, and I fell in love with Africa while reading Mbopo's description of the Zulu way of life—and death. On the few occasions that I was on my own down the Outlaws Wood or up the Fern Wood, I became Umslopogaas the Woodpecker, except that I had my spear instead of the rhinohorn axe, and I loped along all our paths hissing 'Usutu' to the invisible enemy. This I kept to myself, because it was so vastly different to Just William and Robin Hood. They were easy to understand, but the Zulus were special. I knew that I would be open to ridicule if I told my friends that I was Usmlopogaas, and they were the Wolfman and Xhosa dogs. In fact, I knew that they would disown me. If someone had told me in 1941 that eight years hence I would see all that wonderful Haggard country, come to know a great amount of Zulu history, and actually gaze on what was reputed to be The Woodpecker axe in Bulawayo Museum, I think my head may well have fallen off my shoulders with the sheer weight of happiness. After Nada the Lily, there was She, and King Solomon's Mines. Our humble Reading Room was a treasure trove of fine books.

As the hay season arrived, village activity increased. More waggons lurched along the lanes, more men cycled and walked here and there to assist a neighbour in the gathering of the crop. We sped down the steeper slopes of shining hay, perched on large sacks held tight against our feet, and had hay fights, thrusting handfuls down each other's pullovers. We were not yet allowed to handle pitchforks in the field, but our help was welcomed on the waggons, where we flopped about and made the load even, with a hollow in the middle, as the hay was forked up to us. The men never stripped to the waist. They wore collarless shirts with rolled-up sleeves, and some even wore cloth caps with the peak pulled low over their eyes to keep out the glare of the sun, and they worked rhythmically with their pitchforks, smoothly drawing and gathering and lifting, chatting as they harvested the long wide swathes. The horses stood quietly, heads drooping moving forward a few slow paces to a low command, knowing when to stop, without a hand to lead them. And the flies buzzed, annoying the horses and the men and us, and the cattle in the fields, for nowhere in Great Britain, it seemed, were there more flies than around Capel Newydd.

> *Thursday, August 7th. Fine weather. Dai and I saw Major Edwards in his car. Did stripping nettles at school. Melva Lawless and Dorothy and Mair George went up the Frenni Fawr and we saw them on the top from our backway.*
> *Friday, August 8th. Went down Ffynone Garden for Mrs Bigg and earned 6d. Also 6d for some jam jars. Bob, a convalescent, gave me a drawing. Dai found a wasp's nest.*

We often saw the convalescents, distinct in their blue jackets and trousers, white shirts with red ties. We imagined them dented with bullet holes, ravished by scars. They came up most evenings to the Arms and had sing-songs, and walked in pairs down the lanes, winking at us when we stared at them. They never looked ill. We watched a very tall convalescent standing by the stile to Cilgwyn field, drawing Frenni Fawr on a small piece of paper resting on a board. We gradually made contact with him, playing about near him initially, edging nearer, then finally looking over his shoulder by having a piggy-back fight. We began a conversation, discovered that his name was Bob and that he drew things all the time. Did we draw? 'Yeah, but not as good as that. Cor, good, innit?' Bob gave me the drawing, and I kept it for more than twenty years before it faded beyond recall, severing the tenuous link I had with 6287650 Pte Howes of the Buffs Depot, Canterbury. I sometimes wonder if he survived the war.

> *Saturday, August 16th. Don and I went mushrooming with Megan at 6 o'clock in the morning. Went down Ffynone Farm with Dai and Ron. Dai found a nest of baby rabbits. Earned 2d off Mrs Morgan. Don went to Crymmych to meet his mother and father and brother.*

81

There was great expectancy in the shop, and a lot of hustle and bustle, and a flicking of dusters here, there and everywhere. I had to keep out of the way. When Donald's parents and his younger brother arrived it was to a backroom shining with welcome, for his father was a Petty Officer in the Navy, a real serviceman who had seen action on the high seas. He looked splendid in his beribboned uniform, and I am certain that the women in the village sighed at the sight of him. They stayed a few days in the area, visiting the village to say their farewells, and did not take Donald back with them; our Gang was still intact.

During this short period when I was left to my own devices I went on the rounds with Mr Thomas. He stopped at the entrance to one smallholding and said to me, 'Now then, Dick, I don't want you staring or laughing here. Look, but be serious. This lady by here has pearl button teeth, made them herself, she did.'

As I started to laugh he gave me a dig on the arm and said, 'Hisht, nowr te!' and we went into the yard. I saw the lady with the pearl button teeth, stout and ancient, smiling brilliantly with pale blue teeth. They weren't funny; they were lovely.

Friday, August 24th. What has six eyes and can't see? Three blind mice. Joke from the Dandy.
Monday, August 25th. Dull weather. Helped Mr Thomas to rope his onions. Showed Don round Ffynone Farm. Gerwyn and I killed a rat. Started to make a wooden aeroplane. Megan gave me some snaps.
Friday, August 29th. Went to Aberporth with the Church Treat. Good fun there. Won a race. Lost my purse, but not my money. Went in for a swim with Ron Baker.

Our church treat to Aberporth turned out to be an hilarious affair. We were a bus load of whooping kids kept in check by Mr Edwards Pentre. We had picnic lunch and tea, and races on the sands. One race in particular was the main event, involving every boy and girl, and I doubt if Aberporth ever saw such a delightfully chaotic stampede. The forty of us, ranging in age from ten to thirteen, were eventually organised behind a squiggly line drawn in the sand with a stick. Anybody could win because our champion runner, Beckett, who was to become nationally famous later on, was not here, and thank heavens for that.

'Now see over by there?' shouted Mr Edwards pointing to two distant figures spaced well apart on the other side of the little bay, 'That's the finish, in between John and Elfyn. Now then, when I say go, off you go. Ready, then? W-a-i-t, w-a-i-t, OFF!'

And off we went, yelling and screaming, boots and shoes kicking up the fine sand, brown knees pounding, girls' skirts and dresses billowing, people on the side cheering and waving handkerchiefs, and I think we acquired a few additional rogue sprinters as we sped by them, such was the spirit of the event. Donald was behind me. 'Go on, Dick,' he panted with mirth, 'Go on!' I thought I was holding him back, so I put all my energy into sprinting even faster. Out of the corner of my eye I saw the dancing, colourful images of the other racers, fat and thin and short and tall. Then I flew past Elfyn Lewis Yetwen and knew that I had won. I was awarded 6d. and Donald got 3d. and everybody got something, and we all felt marvelous. The money was unimportant—winning was the thing.

Monday, Sept. 1st. Bad weather, rain. After tea, Don and I went to Carregwen to see Mr Lawless making model shoes. Saw a queer caterpillar.

The Lawless girls lived in a pleasant cottage just a few yards from our church of Carregwen. Apart from the Edwards girls, we liked them best. Donald was keen on Melva, the eldest and prettiest. Calling on them to come out to play was out of the question. The girls were not the kind who came out to play. They played tennis. The only way we would ever get to see them would by subterfuge, and Donald hit on the brilliant idea of asking Mr Thomas to ask Mr Lawless if we could come down one evening for instructions in the making of model shoes. Donald said that we were bound to be asked inside. It would be fun, a change. We walked down there in the drizzle.

Mr Lawless did not ask us inside. He was very nice to us, but we had to lean against his wall as he whittled at a piece of wood with his Swiss knife, and made sure that we saw his hands and not his daughters, who were cooped up in the house.

'Pine is nice wood,' he told us. 'Not too soft and not too hard. Easy for your little knife. Now then, if you want to make a tall boot like mine here, then you make sure the grain runs down, but if you want to make a shoe or a clog, then use the grain the other way.' And so he taught us the rudiments of model boot and shoe making, patiently and with pride, for his finished models were perfect, beautifully painted in glossy, flawless Royal Blue. It was unlikely that I would ever emulate him. Donald had quietly disappeared inside with great cunning. I could hear a Victor Sylvester record, a slow waltz, morbid. I envied him his contact with the lovely Lawless girls, and stood quietly fuming as Mr Lawless demonstrated the heel cut with his bone-handled penknife as we stood together by his garden wall in the drizzle. But what I learned that evening I put to good use, and was still making my own model boots forty years later.

Tuesday, Sept 2nd. Letter from Mum and 1/- P.O. Started to make a boot. Dull weather. Dai found a large brown caterpillar.

Wednesday Sept 3rd. Wrote to Mum. Fair weather. Took my clog to the blacksmith to have the iron tightened. Dai caught a small rabbit. We all had fun in the ferns afterwards.

Blackberrying was now officially part of the War Effort. In view of this we were allowed the odd afternoon off from school to contribute and we did it with enthusiasm and style. Many of our local lanes bulged with blackberry bushes, and it was a good year. We used large sweet jars from the shop, Donald and I, and in three days and two evenings we had filled our old bathtub in the shed. Frank and Donald and I waited at the bus stop with pride, the tub at our feet. It was going on the bus free of charge because it was classified War Effort, and Gwyn the bus driver told us the maggots were getting a free ride, too. At the WVS Centre at Boncath the blackberries weighed 25½ lbs. for which we were paid 3/3d. Unfortunately, so many were squashed in the bottom that we must have lost an additional five or six pounds. But it was well worth it, and we had a laugh

84

carrying the empty bath the two miles back to Capel Newydd, in time for bath night on Sadurday. Everywhere one went there were people picking blackberries; it seemed such an easy way to help win the war.

Donald and I were pretending to be Robin Hood, armed with our leaping poles which could serve as a stave in the event of contact with the enemy. With them we leapt gates, crossed fields from molehill to molehill, cleared small rivers and ravines, leapt over bushes, and swiped flat all the thistles and nettles that we could. On this beautiful, simmering, gnat-showered evening we were ambling along the top lane, intending to end up wherever we stopped. A pony appeared over the hilltop, a pony with a larger rider, the unmistakable figure of Muriel Mawr—Big Muriel. We stopped, leaned on our poles in the best Robin Hood fashion, and watched her approach with interest. Muriel seemed lost to the world, making no signs of having seen us, and she was whistling tunelessly.

Donald said to me under his breath, 'Hey, Dick, stop her. Go on, I dare you—make out you're the Sheriff of Nottingham!' and he shook with mirth at his joke. I smiled thinly at him. 'O.K.' I said, 'you watch.'

Without giving the challenge another thought I straightened myself up to look more the size of Litte John, and as Muriel drew level with us I held out my arm. 'Just a mo', I said to her, 'You can't pass here.'

Muriel gave me a look of disdain. 'Why not, then?'

'Because you've got to get off,' I said.

'What's that you was saying', then?' and this time there was a hint of menace in her voice. But I had to go through with this. I was Robin Hood. I repeated the order, squinting up at her against the sun which had set her reddish hair aflame, an omen I failed to take note of—the enemy in the sun. Muriel lifted a great white, knotty-muscled leg over the pony's neck and slid down to the ground with the grace of a sandbag. She took two strides up to me, swung an arm, and slammed me in the face with her fist. There was no warning, no mincing with words. It was a calculated, accurate, intensely hard blow.

85

I think my feet left the ground. In any event, I found myself lying spread-eagled in the lush hedgerow, wild parsley shivering above my eyes in and out of the sun, and myriads of tiny black creatures cascading from the leaves and onto my face. My senses were numbed. I lay there, wondering where my leaping pole was—the weapon that was supposed to safeguard me from this sort of thing—and my face throbbed.

Muriel hauled herself back on to the pony and nonchalantly carried on down the lane, without giving me another glance as far as I can recall, and Donald had disappeared. I struggled up on to shaky legs, alone and half tearful, retrieved my leaping pole lying in the grass, and wandered on up the lane, seeking Donald. By the time I found him waiting for me in the Fern Wood, trying not to look like a coward who has just deserted his best friend in an hour of real need, I had already sorted out Big Muriel, having gone up to her in the playground and pulled her out, screaming, and given her the biggest thrashing she was ever likely to get. 'You wait, I'll get you . . .'

Friday, Sept 5th. Worked at Ffynone Farm on the corn all day. Fine weather. Visited the Ffynone maids. Had my photo taken with Dai and Ron at Ffynone. After tea Ron and I went nutting. Had a tablet. Had to run.
Friday, Sept 19. Sawed logs in the evening. Fine weather. Went weeding at Yetwen in the afternoon. New Library books arrived at school. Mrs Bigg went to SCOTLAND.
Sunday, Sept 21st. Went to church in the morning, and Chapel in the afternoon and evening. After chapel everybody went up the crossroads and sang.

It just happened, and although in retrospect it seemed a wondrous event, I never heard mention made of it afterwards. It was a typical 1941 summer evening, golden, echoing with birdsong, an utterly warless night about to fall. Chapel was over. Adults stood around in chatting knots, all tidy and shiny shoed, and we darted among them like dragonflies in muted game of tag. Slowly, without signal of intent, the small groups joined up, became a purposeful crowd, and there was laughter,

86

and this crowd wended its way up to the crossroads, where it formed a rough circle, blocking the four roads, but there was no traffic so it did not matter. And the crowd sang, men and women, young and old alike, including us, the evacuees. Above and around us the tall trees stood perfectly still, the two pine woods and the two woods of ash, beech and sycamore which were our special haunts, and it was as if they approved and were listening. We sang the favourite, well-known hymns—Calon Lân, Cofia'n Gwlad, Molwn Di, O Dduw Ein tadau. The fervour was extraordinary. As night closed in on us, and the last song died away, and the birds ceased calling, we drifted slowly back to the village, and there were quiet 'Nos Das' as people stopped at their homes or turned down a lane. It never happened again but then real magic happens but once.

Monday, Sept 22nd. Worked down Cilgwyn all day. Fine weather. Don had his first blacksmith's heel irons for his clogs. Had fun in the Fern Wood after tea.

The Fern Wood, so named by us, was very beautiful, an area of thinly spread birch trees in a sea of soft green ferns—candles in a green icing—a place made for children. We had one or two fernhuts still hidden, not yet discovered by the enemy, and in them we often pretended to smoke our elderberry cigarettes. On this particular evening we were crammed in our best hut, Log, Waggy, Eric Thomas, Donald and me. Conversation was trivial. Someone said, 'Let's get Melva.' The idea appealed to us. The more we thought about it, the more fun it seemed. We knew that she was at this very moment taking music lessons at the top school, and would be passing our way in half an hour or so. We feverishly threw out the old ferns in our hut and cut new ones and laid them tidily on the floor, and made the hut outside look more presentable, because there was no doubt in our minds that we would have Melva in here—it was a collective assumption. Gleefully we made it into a love-hut. No plans were laid. 'Getting Melva' was simply a good idea, and getting the fernhouse looking nice was the first stage.

We jogged to the edge of the wood and stood in the tall grass of the verge. From here it was possible to see the schoolhouse and when Melva left we would see her emerge and approach us. We sat down in an excited group, all speaking together. 'I'll have her first!' 'No you won't—I thought of it first,' 'Someone's got to keep guard.' 'Bags I last!'

We began to hide ourselves in the grass and the wild parsley, looking like discarded garden gnomes, tense and eager, while Waggy kept an eye open for Melva's appearance. We had not long to wait. A hiss from Waggy warned us that she was on her way. After a short while we heard a rhythmic squeak. Melva's bike. And she appeared, dark and beautiful, a violin case held precariously in one hand over the handlebar, her slim legs slowly rotated, and when she spotted us cowering in the grass she smiled a dazzling smile and said, 'Hello, boys. There's lovely, isn't it?' And then she was passing us, squeaking her fair way into the sunset, taking her secret body with her.

We stood up, begrimed, armed, clogged and untidy, and looked at the diminishing figure, and at ourselves, and at our spears, and at the lovely sky and trees that filled it, and we ran back whooping and kicked our hut to bits. We threw the ferns at each other, all tension, if indeed there had been any, dissipating in the frantic energy expended as an excuse for failing in our objective. I think we were all relieved that stage two of the plan had not been executed, for none of us would have known what to do next. It was just a game. We suffered no hang-ups, for we were but twelve years old, and far too busy to have worries about girls. They were drips, really.

Tuesday, Sept 23rd. Letter from Mum. Fine weather. Frank and I went nutting in the morning, and blackberrying in the afternoon. Got 9½ lbs. After tea went down Cilgwyn to help.

'Carthorse' and 'Hayseed' were billeted at Cilgwyn Farm. They were very happy there, for the Georges were a warm and generous family, good farmers, popular throughout the area, and we liked old Mr George in particular. We spent a great deal of our spare time at the farm, helping our two classmates with their various tasks. We milked our own favourite cows, hunted the hedgerows for free range eggs, swept out the yard, mucked out the horses, and generally helped where we could. Although we did most of the jobs without thought of payment, because Mrs George always fed us a huge meal, now and again a 6d was thrust into our hands, with token opposition from us. When sheep shearing time came we helped to carry the sheep to the shearers, and three or four hours of sheep heaving had us on our knees. All the shearing was done without electric shears, but we were hard put to keep up with those stolid workers. When it was over for the day we all trooped into the Georges' kitchen, sat round a large table, and had an enormous meal of ham and potatoes and fresh bread with homemade butter, and mugs of sweet tea from an urn on the range. It was different to Ffynone, where no meals were forthcoming now.

Wednesday, Oct 1st. Fine weather. Started to maked an aeroplane for Cyril. In the evening a Whist Drive and Dance was held in the Sessions Room.

On Whist Drive and Beetle Drive and Dance evenings we had to be scrubbed and polished as for Chapel, and succumb to the Mason Pearson torture, and listen to a lecture on how to behave.

Our schoolroom would be miraculously converted within an hour by the redoubtable Thomases, everything disappearing into the corners and on top of each other, leaving plenty of space in the middle for the card tables and chairs. When these were stored out of the way to make way for dancing, one could not see the walls for furniture. We boys quietly infiltrated the room, searching to see which tables contained the interval food, calculating which would be the best one to stand near. We knew almost everyone there, the Davieses Bottom Lodge, Hen Griff y Sir and Billy, Tom and Mair George, the Woold-ridges with Alun looking very smart, Nurse and little Miss Morgan Top Shop, Twm Post and his family, and Evans y Beic without his clips. And Miss Salmon, in revealing dress, showing brown legs and arms, and we couldn't take our eyes off her, because she was very handsome. Altogether, there would be sixty or seventy people, including a fair sprinkling of us boys. We played Whist and Beetles with the grown-ups, and enjoyed the sandwiches and cakes during the interval, but had to leave when the Dance began, so that there was more room. It was usually a very jolly evening. Next morning the room would have been converted back for our use, but cigarette and pipe smoke lingered for days afterwards.

Wednesday, 15th October. Dull weather. Had spelling after school. After tea went about collecting for The Chapel Missionary Society. Got 8/6d.
Thursday, October 16th. Went collecting again. Got 3/9d. Dull weather. Collected another 6d. Stayed in in the evening. Started to wear my winter vest and pants.
Monday, October 20th. Eight Boncath boys joined our class. Ron gave me some glue. Wrote to Paddy Finucane, a crack pilot.

The Boncath boys were an unruly lot. They had not been subjected to our kind of discipline, having had a rather pretty, comparative 'slip of a girl' teacher. They had given her so much trouble that she refused to teach them any longer. There was an emergency meeting between all the local teachers, and they arrived at the solution to this serious problem. Send them to Capel Newydd. We listened to their horrendous tales, and called them liars but believed them nevertheless. Fortunately, they did not spoil us. They could have influenced us with their tales, but the reverse happened. They quietened down, became model pupils, and all was well. All that had been missing in their previous school was discipline and the threat of cane. Also, I like to think that Capel Newydd had a lot to offer in the break periods and lunchtimes, for there were the carpenter's shed and the forge and Cilgwyn lane. It seemed that no other place in Wales could offer these alternatives to bourish behaviour.

Wednesday, October 22nd. Roy Humphries Birthday. Went gardening up the Boncath boys' school in the afternoon. Saw a snake eat a frog.
Sunday, October 26th. Went to Church in the morning. Mrs Thomas Ydlanddegwm gave me a piece of wood to make her a boot.

I recall Mrs T and Y (as we called her) with the deepest affection. She was a widow of many years, for we never heard any reference made to Mr Thomas. Every Sunday morning she came to our shop to sit for a while in the backroom before going off to chapel. She'd come with us, then go to her own pew. She always wore black, at contrast with her red, cheerful face with the little steel glasses. She owned a tiny smallholding on the Llechryd road, which had one fat and affectionate cow, two or three sheep that clambered all over you for food, a few hens, a duck or two, and a magnificent cockerel. Her cottage was half-hidden with creepers, just like the carpenter's shed in Capel Newydd, and at the side was a cattle byre for the solitary cow, and a wood shed absolutely full to the sagging corrugated iron roof with tree branches. It appeared that as the ancient trees on her land died and fell to bits, Mrs T gathered the bits and stored them.

I often went down there in the summer evenings and split logs for her, or did some sawing. She was so sweet to us boys, and always spoke in English. I think she may have been English once upon a time. My abiding memory of Mrs T and Y is when she called me into the cow byre when I was busy sawing logs for her. She proffered me a churn lid of warm, bubbly milk straight from her cow's enormous udder. And it was a drink fit for the gods. 'You'll like this,' she said, 'because it is pure.' I will always remember gasping when I had finished tilting the churn lid, and feeling the bubbles tickle my lips and chin, and wondering why milk didn't always taste like this.

I made a pair of boots for her, and Eirlys found a safety pin for me so that I could present it to her on a little chain for a brooch. I charged her only sixpence, because she had given me the piece of wood from which to carve them; I had decided that my boots would sell for 1/- a pair. She wore them every Sunday when she called in, but out of the corner of my eye I caught her removing them and slipping them into her handbag as we all entered the chapel together.

Friday, Nov 29th. Fine weather. Saw something like a Star shining in the sky. A new Invention called a Shell-Star. Made Xmas Cards in school. Mr Thomas brought a live hen home. Called it Archibald.

Monday, Dec 8th. Japan declared War on America. Fine weather. Started to write a story. My clog heel cracked.

Wednesday, Dec 10th. Dull weather. The Prince of Wales and the Repulse were sunk. I wrote my story. Saw a concert called Bois Y Frenni.

Bois Y Frenni gave a very lively show. We had to admit afterwards that it was better than ours, voicing our opinions in public in the hope that we would be contradicted, but we were not. I still retain a vivid memory of it. A Captain someone-or-other conjured a glass of milk from an empty cardboard cylinder and pulled endless handkerchiefs from his sleeve, bringing the house down with applause. On stage, two men sat on a bench, one of them bemoaning the fact that he was always hungry, never had enough money to buy a drink, hated the sun because it burned his skin, hated the rain because it soaked through his coat, hated the mist over the mountains. 'What about you, now then?,' he asked the other man on the bench, 'Fair play now, there's a lot wrong with the world, isn't there? What do you do, then?' And the other man said, 'Nothing much except enjoy every minute. You see, I'm blind.' There was a silence after this enigmatic reply, then a thunderous applause from the rapt audience. A classical pianist played miraculous music on the stained and chipped and neglected piano which stood in the corner. Finally, a pretty woman mounted the stage and gave us a monologue in loud and clear voice, until she began to forget her lines, whereupon her voice developed a croak, and she began to cough and hold her throat while we all watched her, entranced. One of the Bois came on and led her away with profuse apologies—she had been working too hard all up and down the country, and had this throat disorder, you see—so everybody was very understanding and gave her an ovation. Then an old man sat on a chair on the stage and played all the songs we knew on a huge and ornate accordion, which we all enjoyed enormously, especially 'Sospan Fach,' then both anthems were played and it was all over. And of the hundreds of various shows I have seen in half a dozen countries, that particular one is the one I recall with gladness.

Saturday, Dec 20th. Fine weather. Had a Xmas Card from Lois. Went getting logs with Mr Thomas in the afternoon. In the morning, took my clogs down Abercych. Dai, Log, Frank and Don came with me. Had a ride back on the churn lorry.

The churn lorry was old, and it whined its way up and down the lanes, stopping at every milk-churn stand, unloading empties, taking on the full ones, a tough job for a strong man. It came through the village, up to the cross roads, stopped at a stand nearby, then went in second gear down the hill, loaded to capacity. At a critical stage up the hill it almost stopped as the driver changed gear; it usually shuddered in protest, but just managed to continue its journey. It was at this point that we emerged from our hiding place in the hedge and flung ourselves onto the tailboard, gleefully hoisting ourselves up to get a lift back to the crossroads, where we would drop off before the lorry came to a halt. We had done this once or twice before, and come to no harm.

This time, however, Frank found himself unable to clamber aboard, despite our cries of encouragment, and as the lorry began to accelerate along the straight stretch, Frank's strides became enormous. He began to cover five yards with each stride, making it impossible to haul himself up. All he could do was allow the ground to sweep beneath his ever-increasing leaps, fear brightening his eyes, and we clung to his pullover to prevent him taking off. The lorry began to slow rapidly at the next and final incline before coming to the crossroads. Frank was so exhausted that he let go, his pullover stretching like rubber in our grip, and we released him, watching him collapse in an untidy heap in the road. We all, in loyalty to our fallen comrade, jumped off too, and stood laughing as he dragged himself up after covering the fastest two hundred yards of his life.

Monday, Dec 22nd. Dull weather. Frank's pigs killed. Saw one of them killed. Donald and I had a Xmas Card each. After tea, Frank and I earned 3/4d carol singing.
Wednesday, Dec 24th. Fine weather. First day of the hols. Went carol singing with Frank and Don in the evening and earned 11/-. Got my Clogs back from Abercych.
Dec 25th. Had lots of presents. In the morning went down to Newcastle Emlyn for Dinner and tea. After Tea we went down to Ffynone to a Party.

There was an open invitation to all of us ex-boys to come to the Ffynone Party. We wore our best suits and shoes, and set out happy and excited. Donald was allowed to come because it was inconceivable that I should go and not he. Frank couldn't come as a special guest because there was work to be done—the animals didn't stop eating or drinking just because it was Christmas, did they? So it was working clothes on for Frank, and his yoke and buckets, and many journeys to the village pump in the dark. But he said he'd walk part of the way with us, as far as Yetwen on the straight.

We strode along the dark road. 'Pity you can't come with us, Frank,' I said. 'I reckon you've got a right old faggot there, making you work tonight. Why couldn't Alun do it?' And so we cursed Frank's billetors, who did indeed seem to work him uncommonly hard, as well as their own son, for poor Mr Wooldridge was hampered by his hardening of the lungs. They had half a dozen cows and a few pigs—two less now—but the work they caused seemed out of all proportion; even carrying water the two hundred yards from the pump to the trough took hours, and it was as if the trough had a hole in it.

Frank got more and more despondent. We, his best pals, all neat and tidy about to have a great evening, he in his elbow-worn red pullover and stained trousers and clogs, about to start watering. It didn't seem right. The injustice of it gradually weighed too heavily even for his staunch frame, and he suddenly collapsed into the grass at the side of the road, and he curled into a little ball, and wept. He wept as Eric had wept at the loss of his sister, with a wretchedness that no-one could understand, it was too deep and personal. His grubby little hands clenched themselves over his eyes, and he sobbed, 'It's not fair!' over and over, and all Donald and I could do was shuffle and stand near him and hope that our presence would somehow console him, and we could have wept for him, too. This wasn't in keeping with the spirit of Christmas at all, and we were embarrassed by his grief. But he pulled himself together when he'd had his cry, and wiped his nose on his sleeve and said he'd kick those f----- buckets all the way to the pump. Then he started walking back on his own, swallowed up in the war-black of the night, and all we heard was the clomping of his clogs.

The Party was a huge success, Frank was forgotten in the gaiety and wonder of it all, for those convalescents adored us youngsters and gave us a splendid treat. Sometimes I wonder if they pitied us, despite their own war. If so, they were mistaken, and should have cast their pity into other quarters, for we were intensely happy and content.

The mansion has changed dramatically inside to accommodate the dozens of new inmates who seemed to emerge from every room, looking very fit, with only a few plastered limbs and crutches.

Everything was going on in the vast drawing room, which had been forbidden territory in our day. A darts tournament was in progress, with a prize for the highest score of the evening, and there was quoit throwing into a crêpe-covered bucket. An impressively large sideboard held bottles of beer and lemonade and plates of sandwiches and sausage rolls, Welsh cakes and biscuits, dates and grapes and apples and bananas. We had a quick game of Beetle Drive in which almost everyone cheated, and a very successful game of Charades. Daniel Daniels, Esq. J.P. and Mrs Daniels and Mrs Bickerton-Edwards appeared and disappeared like happy ghosts, and Mr Dunne the butler was there with the little white towel over his arm, looking very pleased with himself, and not a little tipsy. One game I remember was called the Egyptian Mummy. We were led one at a time into the drawing room, in subdued light, on the floor of which lay a figure shrouded with a sheet, only the shoe-clad feet showing. This, we were informed in reverent tones, was the 'Mummy', capable of granting any wish within reason. All you had to do was kneel with your head on the floor, bottom in the air, and ask your wish, facing the head of the Mummy—you musn't talk to its feet. On uttering your wish, the feet of the Mummy swiftly became an arm, and the shoe rapped you firmly on the behind, to the delight of the watchers, and taking you completely by surprise. Then there was the Lift, whereby the Lift ascended slowly with the help of two brawny and obviously very fit convalescents. The person on the lift, blindfolded, was quite certain that he was being lifted a few feet off the ground. When the lift descended—it was a short, wide plank of wood—the victim was told to jump because the lift was on fire. A mighty leap into space, only two or three inches above the ground, brought one to an abrupt halt, and the victim was awarded a bar of chocolate for putting up with the back-breaking jar with such good humour.

We had an hilarious time, and hugged the maids who told us, 'There's tall you are getting—you'll all be men soon!' Lovely girls.

When it was all over, and we were scruffy with the exertion of it all, and feeling quite tired, the anthems were sung with tremendous feeling, and we walked home. I think it was the best Christmas Donald and I had ever had.

> *Friday, December 26th. Played up the crossroads all afternoon. Collected kindling in the pony field. Went down to Penfedw after tea and got 1/- each from Mrs Thomas there.*
> *Saturday, Dec 27th. Dull weather. Helped Frank to carry water most of the day. Played with my leaping pole.*
> *Wednesday, Dec 31st. Fine weather. Heavy frost. Played up the crossroads in the afternoon. Not much to do after tea. Wore my helmet.*

And so the year ended. We did not stay up till midnight to see the New Year in, for this was not considered to be an especially exciting affair while a blackout was imposed. After nightfall it was as if each family was cocooned, isolated by the uncompromising dark. Also, if what the adults said was true, there was not too much to shout about, for the war was not going our way just now. We did not involve ourselves with the war business, insulating ourselves from it with our gift for devising our own amusements with what was available.

My first diary was full of inconsequential events, and useless bits of information. With a miserly bent I had recorded my costs for the year. 2/- on church collections, 2/6 on snaps, and 9/- on my clogs. I had received eleven free bars of chocolate for working in the garden and sawing logs. And I put 2/6 in National Savings. My total earnings for 1941 were 40/-, mainly due to the unfailing generosity of the locals, who paid us for the most trivial messages.'

And Don loves Anita Baugh. Eric loves Barbara Lockyer. Ron loves Megan Jenkins. Carthorse loves Muriel Reece. Waggy loves Vida Eden. I love Dorothy Edwards.

1942
January 1st, Thursday. Dull weather. Went round the houses saying Happy New Year. Don and Ian Lockyer came. Earned

1/4d. Chapel in the afternoon. Went to the Chapel Treat. Very good. Had a Testament Newydd. Dai's Birthday.

One of the chapel's endearing efforts was to reward those youngsters who had served it most faithfully by attending every Tuesday evening Bible Class and Sunday afternoon chapel. Donald and I were in no position to refuse the challenge, nor would we really have refused to attend had we the choice, because they were cosy affairs. All the boys sat on one side of the pews, and all the girls on the other, and hands shot into the air in competition to answer the questions put to us by the tall and graceful Mair George on Tuesday evenings, and Griff y Sir on Sunday afternoons. We learned very quickly to read Welsh, for there were no English editions. Each attendance was confirmed by a colourful biblical stamp in our books, and I recall the simple pleasure these gave us.

Presentations were given after the Chapel Treat, one of the many Treats we enjoyed in the Christmas and New Year period; we always seemed to be dressing up and getting brushed and running off to a Treat. Even the name Treat seemed better than Party. The New Testament, with name engraved, was a sought-after possession. After all, it was forever, for keeps, to be handed down to one's children. It was the Best Prize. Three or four of us won these—neither Donald nor I because our allegiance was shared by Carregwen—and then there were the books. All the grown-ups applauded each award. No one left empty handed, for that was not the way things were done in chapel.

Friday, Jan 9th. Played football with Don and Frank and the Yetwen boys after tea. Had a short lecture from Mr Hawkins for messing about in school. Had a ride on Ian Lockyer's bike. Eirlys' Birthday.
Saturday, Jan 10th. Fine weather. Washed the pony trap, then went down Ffynone Farm with Dai and Ron. In the afternoon Dai and Frank and I went Paper Salvage collecting. Got a good lot.

Save Paper was the new War Effort. We had done exceptionally well with the nettles and the blackberries, so we resolved to excel at this paper campaign too. And there was money to be earned at it. My roller skates were no longer safe to skate on, the rough roads having torn the rims, so we dismantled them into their four parts, and screwed them on to the four corners of a good piece of wood, nailed four sides to it, attached a rope, and we had a truck. Initially our journeys were short ones, covering the village, and in no time at all we had our first few loads; money for old rope. All the old magazines came out, and journals, books, comics, newspapers. Every house donated its rubbish gladly. It was when we began the farm journeys that we found it hard work, for the small wheels of our truck soon clogged up with mud, and we were forever upending it to clear the mud off. But we collected an enormous pile, which was again stored in the big shed at Pentre after being picked up from school.

Sunday, Jan 11th. Went to Chapel in the morning and each of us had an Album. Also went to chapel in the afternoon and evening. Crymmych Home Guard had a fight with ours. We won. Saw a black rabbit.

We knew that if the crunch ever came, we could rely on our village Home Guard, stalwarts all; Tom George Cilgwyn, Billy ifanc and Mr Wooldridge, Mr Evans Tavern and Jack y Tractor, Mr Thomas Stiff Leg, Evans y Lodge and Griff y Gardd, and Mr Parry the schoolmaster officer in charge. There were others, too, from around, but we did not know them well enough to say ''Hello'' to. Their parade ground was the area by the pump in front of the Arms, only a right turn from the front door and inside. Only two Lee Enfield rifles were allocated to our unit, and they were shared. Clad in ill-fitting khaki, gaiters, and shiny boots and forage caps splitting their heads in half, they 'shunned' and 'present arms'-ed and 'bout turn'-ed one evening every week while we stood back and admired their prowess.

'There's smart is Griff, eh?' 'There's a lovely attention, isn't it?' 'Fair play, now, the boys are very good, aren't they?'

On occasions there would be night exercises against other troops, and we would see shadowy figures flitting about the hedges trying to tip-toe silently down the street, hiding in doorways, and would hear hoarse commands in loud whispers. Now and then one of the rationed flares would go off, illuminating the scene with frightening brilliance, and thunder flashes caused the cows and ponies to bellow and neigh, adding to the confusion. When the exercise was over the Tavern became full.

Monday, Jan 17th. Rotten weather. Had the cane off Mrs Bigg. Took my clogs to the smithy. Did my Warships Weekly Advertisement at home.
Thursday, Jan 29th. I had a notice that my painting had passed the Warships Weekly Competition. I was the only one out of all the Hythe school. Played football with the Welsh boys after school. They won.

Mr Hawkins had kept me back after school for another lecture, to be followed by the cane; this was obvious by the way he opened the top of the cupboard in the corner and took it out. He told me things about myself which I had never dreamed of. I lacked application. I was very bright but I digressed. I showed off. I was not a good example. All I ever seemed to want to do was to play about, and it was not good enough. Perhaps this would teach me to pull myself together . . . Just as he flexed the cane, Donald burst into the room. 'Sir, Dick's won, sir!'
Mr Hawkins stayed his upraised arm. 'Won what, Beagley?'
'The ship competition sir! For the school, sir!'
Mr Hawkins was delighted. He spared me the cane, and while he did not exactly hug me in triumph for the school, he smiled and said what a good effort; see? I could do well when I wanted to. It was not a terribly prestigious win, but it was a good one in view of the competition, and I had the immense pleasure of seeing my painting as a stamp, along with winners from other, better schools. I can remember the elation I felt on running down to the shop to see the letter. The war was terrific.

Monday, Feb 9th. Megan went to Haverfordwest for good. Pony had new front shoes.
Saturday, Feb 14th. Fine weather. In the morning got five sacks of wood on our truck. In the afternoon went tracking. Brought Mr Jones Cilrhiwfach's pony to the blacksmith for

shoeing. Dug a bit in the garden after tea, also played football.
Megan came home for the week-end.

We knew Mr Jones's pony well. Dwts, a fat little thing with a
bent back and sturdy legs. One of our treats was to go to
Cilrhiwfach on an evening and give her some exercise. Mr
Jones only kept her in the tiny field at the back of his farm to
keep the grass down, because she was too small to pull anything, but he did not have the heart to part with her. Twm
Llewellyn told us that Mr Jones, despite his rough appearance,
was a kindly man who had rescued Dwts from a bad home.
Donald and I used to saddle her up then ride her up and down
the little field in turns. Dwts never ran in the direction away
from the farm buildings, only when she was turned round to
face them, when she got up quite a canter. After an hour of this
she was decidedly slimmer, and Mr Jones was pleased that we
had all enjoyed ourselves. Not that he could speak for Dwts.

Sunday, Feb 15th. In the morning went to church. Fine
weather. In the afternoon a lot of us boys had three rides in
some Bren gun carriers of the Army. They stopped at the
village, and so we didn't go to chapel. Went to chapel in the
evening.

There were half a dozen of the carriers, efficient, noisy little
things in olive green, with rolled up camouflage nets in the
back. They were manned by about twenty bright-faced, happy
young soldiers. We crowded around the vehicles, the first we
had ever touched or seen, and to our astonishment the soldiers
offered to give us rides up and down the village street. I can
remember the women laughing in little groups outside the shop
as we rattled past them up to the crossroads and back again,
waving and cheering and thrilled. Later, when the men had
covered the backs of the vehicles up, and were seated on packs
strewn along the verge sipping tea, one of them asked me who
Eirlys was. 'Eirlys,' I told him, giving the correct pro-
nunciation, which to him must have sounded like Ay-rrr-liss.
'Who's she when she's at home?'
'ILLIS,' I repeated, so that he could understand. He wrote
her a little note, which I passed on to her later on. There was no

100

reply, only a laugh. The soldiers camped in one of the fields for the night, the carriers drawn up in a tidy line by the roadside, and when Don and I went to get Bess the next morning, they had gone, and it was as if they had never been. It was the first time that we had had contact with real fighting soldiers, and wished they could come back again. They had been really nice to us.

Thursday, Feb 17th. Wrote to Dorothy. Cut a leg off a dead owl, and am keeping it for luck, and took a feather. Went to chapel in the evening. Fell in love with Dorothy Edwards.

This was the real thing. A chance encounter, a radiant smile outside the village shop, and I was smitten with love for Dorothy. In between making camps and barricades, cutting spears and bows and arrows, painting, and sawing logs and designing aeroplanes, she occupied my thoughts to an alarming degree. I even had a letter from her, handed to me in secret by one of her friends during the lunch hour, asking if I would be at church next Sunday.

Monday, March 2nd. Mr Hawkins taught us at school. Mrs Bigg ill in bed. Washed down pony trap because Mr Thomas had to take a coffin down to Abercych. After tea played with the boys up the crossroads.
Saturday, March 28th. Mr Hawkins and family went back. Salvaged at Yetwen in the afternoon and took it up the school house. Stayed in after tea and painted. Megan came home.

The headmaster and Mrs Hawkins and Lois stayed at the Arms on their final evening, and the little Austin was allowed to park on our shop yard at the side. We had mixed emotions about their departure. Not too unhappy about the headmaster leaving, because he did keep a very tight rein on us, but we would be sorry to see Mrs Hawkins leave, and especially Lois. The last we saw of them on Sunday morning was them waving from CKR 724 as she snorted in the cold air down the village street. They left an emptiness behind.

With Mrs Bigg ill in bed, speculation was rife. The Boncath Lot said they'd go and fetch the pretty girl teacher they had so distressed a few months ago. We thought we might get a teacher from Cardigan who could teach us rugby. We even thought we might be amalgamated with the top school, and I nearly fainted at the thought of sitting in close proximity to Dorothy, perhaps even at the same desk. In the event, none of these fantasies were even close to the real solution. We got Mr Bigg. The hard man.

I recall Mr Bigg as a lean and bespectacled figure in bicycle clips, with a thin, humourless face, in thick tweeds, like Mrs Bigg used to wear. They both must have suffered from the cold. He had a rasping voice that spelled the end of singing lessons. When he spoke there seemed to be ice on every word. Somehow, I thought, we aren't going to have an easy time with this man. Nor did we. He was uncompromising with the cane, almost brutal. But he was a splendid teacher. He produced from us a phenomenal work rate. His stern order to 'Get your head down' was never questioned. He was an excellent maths teacher who thrust basic trigonometry upon us in no time. He loved books, so instead of singing we had reading which was more interesting. Now and again he smiled, and it was like the sun breaking through heavy clouds. If he was a hard man, then there were cracks in the concrete, and we could be grateful for that. (Many years later I had tea with him in his flat. Mrs Bigg had passed on, his two children grown up and gone their separate ways, and he was on his own. He surprised me greatly by telling me that his posting to Capel Newydd was one of the nicest things that had ever happened in his teacher's role. He had enjoyed our company.)

Megan came home most week-ends from her telephonist job at Haverfordwest, and Donald and I looked forward to these visits because the likelihood was that we could ride her bike. It was an impressively fine bike, a curved-frame Hercules, with corded rear mudguard and a full chainguard, and fat purring tyres. Riding on it was different to anyone else's bike we could borrow. We kept it clean and never rode it without her consent. She would think of messages to give us so that we could give the bike an airing, taking it in turns to ride to Abercych or Boncath or Llechryd, or wherever. Once, I sped to Boncath on an errand and saw my friends by the little station. The barrier was down, as a train was expected through. On an impulse I cycled hard towards them, applying the brakes so that I could execute a spectacular skid, and they would all say, 'Wow!' Unfortunately, the front brake was more efficient than the rear one, and I hurtled over the handlebars and into the barrier netting, and slumped to the ground like a rag doll, sending the bike spinning and clattering. I was horrified at the apparent damage—twisted handlebars and a pedal embedded in the chainguard. My torn trousers and cut knees were insignificant by comparison.

We picked up the bike, and after a brief discussion it was wisely decided to take it to the blacksmith. I do not remember him, but he was marvellous, and I remember him telling me that this would teach me to show off, wouldn't it, now then, eh? then a laugh, and 'Let's have a look at her,' and we stood in a circle round him, willing him to perform a miracle. And he did. With his God-given gift of metal-knowledge he tapped out the dent in the chainguard after removing the pedal, and he made the pedal stem right angled again, and twisted the handlebars back between his knees, and even dabbed shiny black paint here and there. When he had finished we all sighed 'Wow!' for there were no indications of accident damage. I thanked him in my best Welsh. Everyone swore that Megan would not hear of the incident from *their* lips. I rode the bike home carefully, speaking tender words to it all the way, apologising, and swearing never to do things like that again, not on her anyway. No one at home ever heard of the accident.

Tuesday, April 7th. Fairly good weather. Visited my mice. Both escaped. Don had notice that he could go home with Mrs Parks. He gave me a jig-saw and a book and a pen. After tea went to chapel. Wrote today's diary with Don's pen.
Saturday, April 12th. Nice weather. Went potato planting at Penralltgoch all day from 10 till 5.30. Don had a letter. After tea went down to Pentre.

Many of the villagers hired a part of a potato field on one of the farms. It was a source of income to the farmer, and of benefit to the villager. Seed potatoes were cheap, and the

103

return could be prolific. In 1942 Twm Llewellyn hired two long rows at Penralltgoch. Donald and I helped the Lewises to plant their field all day, and we planted our two rows at the same time. We weren't paid, so it would be fair to assume that our labour was a payment in kind between Twm and the Lewises.

We enjoyed planting potatoes. We wore a sack round our waists, held at two corners to form a basket, and when this was filled from a sack on the tailboard of one of the gambos, we trooped to our row and pressed a potato into the ground at every clog interval. Now and again we'd throw a potato at each other, or at someone else, or tell one of the other boys that he was in the wrong row, and giggleavingle at the confusion this caused. The weather was usually quite lovely, so that we could wear just our pullovers instead of a sack over our shoulders. Lunch was brought out on a float or a gambo, and there would always be the scalding hot tea in thick white mugs.

> *Tuesday, April 14th. Fine weather. In the afternoon we all did the garden up Mr Baugh's house. In the evening, went down Cilgwyn for a short while. Went to chapel also. FRANK WENT HOME. Ken Tugwell's mother came down.*

This was traumatic for Donald and me. Our gang had not long been sworn in again—it was resworn everytime someone joined, Waggy being the last member—and now Frank was leaving; he was a founder member. Ginger, when we were Just William, Friar Tuck when we were Robin Hood. His going hit us badly. We were so used to helping him out in the evenings with his tasks that it was part of our way of life. And you couldn't find anyone to replace Frank, not actually *replace* him; only make the number up again. We'd have to see about Eric Thomas, Mr Stiff Leg's son, because we got on well with him. Gosh, fancy Frank going . . .

> *Tuesday, April 21st. Fairly good weather. In the afternoon worked up the school garden. After tea, worked in our garden and went to chapel. Found a moorhen's nest at Wendros pond. 6 eggs.*

Wendros pond lay at the side of the road halfway to Boncath, a mysterious litle pond, towered over on one side by the thin

104

silent pine trees of the lower spinney. It was surrounded by tall reeds, and the cottage of Danny and his wife squatted close by. It was an old, red brick, slate-roofed, criumbling little cottage. Danny was in the army. When he came home on his first leave he strode up to the village to see everyone and for everyone to see him in his uniform, and he proudly told us of the work his regiment did, like digging latrines and clearing woods. Look, our badge has an axe on it. He had been drafted into the Pioneer Corps, and Danny thought the world of the regiment. None of us boys could understand why the grown-ups thought it was so funny. Danny also owned the only motorcycle in the district, even if he was a laugh. It was probably an Aerial, with water-cooled radiator. One evening he roared up the village on it, and gave Donald and me a long ride each on the back, an exhilarating experience. We boys thought Danny Wendros was terrific. (I hope he survived the war.)

Friday, April 24th. The school went potato planting at Cilrhiwfach. We all earned 2/- each.
Saturday, April 25th. Fine weather. In the morning went with Don to meet his father. DON WENT BACK. Ron Butler's father came down and RON WENT BACK. Worked all afternoon at Penfeddw and earned 1/-.

I cannot remember Donald actually leaving Capel Newydd. However, I remember the desolation I felt when I worked all that long hot afternoon at Penfeddw, a highly organised farm with a prize-herd of cattle. My task was to sweep the yard. It was a large yard, and the dust lay thick. I was in no mood for doing anything but to reflect on how badly things were going. My world of make-believe was falling apart. You couldn't possibly have a gang without Frank and Don. And what about the garden at the shop? I'd have it all to do myself, and when Evans y Beic leaned over the hedge and had a chat with Mr Thomas, I'd have no one to laugh with, no more jokes about shiny waistcoats and bicycle clips. And at bedtime, I'd have to read by myself, and not suddenly burst out with, 'Hey, listen to this . . . !' And Chapel. It was going to be terrible without Don. I'd be the only English boy there now. There seemed no end to the gloom that had settled over my life.

105

I collected my shilling and trudged home. I passed the vicarage, hands in my pockets, head hung in despondency. I could feel myself becoming choked. On an impulse I stumbled over the hedge and into the ash wood opposite the vicarage, flung myself down at the foot of one of the trees, and burst into tears. All kinds of images fled swiftly through my mind; the Outlaws wood, baths of blackberries, secret fernhuts, all shared things. I knew with a child's instinct that things were never to be the same again, that from the moment when I stepped into the shop in quarter of an hour's time, I was going to have to face up to the fact that the games were over. I wept fiercely and bitterly for lost times, and my new loneliness. The despair I felt, however, lasted but two or three days, for children are blessed with a resilience of which they are unaware.

Waggy moved into the village from bottom lodge, because Mrs Evans was unwell and felt unable to cope. He billeted with the Thomases of the Reading Room. Their son Eric was our age, but better than us—he went to Cardigan Grammar School. We decided that he was good enough to be part of our gang, provided that he passed the Tests down the Outlaws Wood, which he did with ease. The evenings were no longer the same without Donald, and I often found myself in the woods on my own after I'd done a bit of gardening. It was not much fun, stretching credulity to the full pretending to be hunted by someone who was not there. I asked Mr Bigg if I could do homework. He was surprised, then pleased. Everyone was suprised and pleased.

Friday, May 8th. Fine weather. Worked all day setting potatoes at Cilgwyn and earned 1/3d. Had a letter from Don. Had a haircut from Johnnie the postman.
Saturday, May 9th. Fine weather. In the evening went with Mr Thomas on the pony and trap to get bean sticks. Got 51 over by Wendross. After tea got a Buzzard's egg and a crow's egg. Megan came home.

The garden required considerable attention at this time of the year, and I found it taking more and more of my time. I loved the garden, which was fortunate, or I may well have rebelled. Everything in it was bigger and better than anyone

106

else's, due to the care lavished on it and the help from Bess. I seemed to draw closer to the family. They certainly treated me as a son, and my Welsh became quiet fluent and my vocabulary greatly expanded. I went with Twm Llewellyn up to the Chapel House to sit with him and tiny Mr Lewis to hear Winston Churchill speak to the nation. The old men stared at each other through clouds of pipe smoke as the great man spoke. I was too young to grasp the flavour of the moment, only appreciating it years later, for the speech became famous. When it was over Twm Llewellyn smiled in triumph, and I do not doubt for one moment that he was inspired by those grand words. 'Duw! What a man, eh? Of course you know that he's half-Welsh—the best half?' When we walked back down the street, his leg creaking and my clogs clicking, he put his arm around my shoulder and said, 'It won't be long now, Dick bach, and you'll be able to go home.' But I didn't want to go home just then. My marrows were growing well.

Hayseed was now on his own too, at Cilgwyn Farm, so I spent longer hours down there helping him. At school there were only six of the original Newchapel Boys, all the others having gone home with their parents. We were swamped by the Boncath Lot. On May 1st, Dai went home, and I never saw him again.

Saturday, June 20th. Lovely weather. All morning till 1 o'clock six of us worked in Ffynone field thinning out sugar beet. Earned 1/6d. Afterwards went to see the maids at the mansion and then had a look round the farm. Just played about after tea by myself.
Wednesday, July 1st. In the morning we all went collecting foxglove leaves down Pentre way.

The new clarion call was for Digitalis, a drug derived from the foxglove. Once again our academic hours were curtailed in favour of assisting in the War Effort. Cilgwyn lane was for nettles, Pentre lane and Cilwendeg Drive were for foxgloves. This was the best work yet, and once again we were to be paid for it. My experience as Master Raker for nettles assured me the similar job down the Pentre shed for foxglove leaves. Further, Mr Bigg would loan me his tall black bike to ride down every-

107

day and do my job. All we had to do was pick off the leaves from the plants, like tea plantation workers, and we carried satchels to put them in, and we stuffed them down each others neck when Mr Bigg wasn't looking. They were lovely days.

Wednesday, July 22nd. Rotten weather. Rain all day. Turned the leaves over at Pentre in the dinner hour. Wrote to Mum. After tea, Eric Turner, Peter West, Freddie and I went in Mr Williams (Blaenffos) car to Crymmych and had our cadet uniforms.

We met at the sombre hall where we had first disembarked more than two years ago as children. Now, we were suddenly young men, thrust into the uniformed world of the soldier. I have no idea how we came to know of the Army Cadet Force, but it was probably by a circular through the schools. The following evening Eric and I met at Tanrhiw, and we strode along the lanes in step, forage caps sitting squarely, collars draining the blood from our throats, the coarse material chaffing the insides of our thighs, and boots squeaking. I can still recall the new smell of that uniform, and the tight feel of it. We called at Ffynone to see the maids again, and they gaped at us and said, 'Duw! where have the little boys gone, now then?' Where had they gone?

Saturday, July 25th. Fine weather. In the morning made a camp up the woods by myself. In the afternoon got a sack full of leaves and took them down to Pentre and turned the others over. In the evening played down Cwmfelyn and Cilgwyn dingle by myself.

One of the extraordinary features of our part of Wales was the contrast in the living conditions. Some farms were squalid, the farmer uncouth, sometimes brutal to his animals. They were the exception, but they nevertheless existed, and were avoided by us. You could sense the hostility by the manure-defiled doors, the dirty, broken gates, and the piles of junk in the nettlebeds, the state of the roofs. On the other hand, the farms with which we were in daily contact were clean, despite the muddied yards. The farm houses were bright and warm and you could eat off the polished floors even though chickens came in and out all day. The farmers' wives would hand us still-hot Welsh cakes straight off the oven top, and the lace curtains moved mist-like at the small square windows. There was a beautiful smell of ham and new bread and tea and milk. In nearly all the farm houses the butter was made in the adjoining dairy, hams were hung up stiff and white with salt, and a tea urn sizzled on the oven all day long, while aromatic bread rose within the oven.

The wives worked intensely hard. They had their hair tied back out of the way, and wore loose dresses and aprons. Black stockings made their legs appear thick and they had clogs on their feet. Their hands were lined and hard with pail carrying and fork wielding, with chicken plucking and stove raking, with men's work. They not only shared the farm load, they set to in their own houses, without help from their menfolk, scrubbing, polishing, cleaning, cooking, churning, and yet they welcomed us cheerfully into their houses when we called, as if they had expected us.

But on Sundays they were suddenly transformed. Gone the aprons and clogs, the bustling and scurrying in and out of the house to the sheds. Instead, a sedate walk up the chapel path, scrubbed hands clasping a Testament Newydd, flower-topped hat shading a Palmolive holy face, legs slendered in lisle stockings, feet smaller in patent leather shoes. And beside them, or behind, slow-striding husbands, trussed in tight fitting blue serge and uncomfortable, shiny white collar round red, turkey neck, with squeaking boots, blue eyes alert, hands behind back, already impatient for the end of the service so that they could get back to the cows.

Monday, August 3rd. Fine weather. In the Afternoon we all went to Pentre and packed the foxglove leaves up. Got 66lbs. After tea we had Cadet practice up Crymych. Had another fight with Alun Wooldridge and gave him a lip bleed.

The Cadet Force took up an increasing amount of our spare time. We were quite proud of the awful, capacious garment

109

that encased us and which passed as a uniform. It made us part of the War, activists, men set aside from those children who pulled salvage along the village street on an old roller skate truck, or carried baths of blackberries to the Boncath WVS. We were soldiers now.

Eric and I were blatant swanks. We paraded openly in the village street now before being picked up by our Officer, Mr Williams the headmaster at Blaenffos. (All the headmasters automatically became Officers.) No more keeping to the country lane for us. One evening, when we were strutting like bantam cockerels along the street, in step, I saw Alun Woold-ridge laughing at us behind his hand. I ordered him to tell me what was so funny. He called out that we couldn't stop a blind man coming up the street, never mind a German. He was going to change sides. I walked up to him and hit him in the face, a churlish thing to do, and he toppled backwards over our wall and onto the lawn. There was a shriek behind us as his mother, witness to my assault, dropped everything to get at us, clenched fist in the air. Eric and I turned and fled, all dignity forgotten, and with sterling effort we gained the safety of the fields, thence down to the bottom lodge where we could wait for Mr Williams to pick us up, and our crotches itched cruelly from the rubbing of that coarse army material.

Wednesday, August 5th. First day of summer hols. Lovely weather. Letter and 2/- from Mum. From 12.30 to 9 o'clock Eric Thomas and Waggy, Maggie Bigg and Beryl and Eric Turner and Ian Lockyer and I went to Poppit on bicycles and had a swim. Eisteddfod at Cardigan began.
Friday, August 7th. Rotten weather. Rain all day. In the morning I finished making my truck. In the afternoon I went out by myself salvaging and Ian came with me. Worked in the garden after tea then played with Ian. Last day of Eisteddfod. Time put back one hour.
Monday, August 17. Fine weather. I, Ian Lockyer, Eric Thomas and Babs Lockyer went Flax Picking all day at Newport. We went there and back in the buses. Trixie my pigeon died. Megan went up to Aunt Liz at Castell Newydd Emlyn.

I think that a flax field is one of nature's special ceremonial robes. Few sights are as beautiful as a flax field ready for harvesting, with the sun and soft breeze giving the impression of a golden sea full of motion. We had never seen flax before, and I have not seen it since. We were, I think, privileged to help in its harvesting, along with about a hundred other school children. The farmer demonstrated how to pull a handful out near the roots, tapping it against one's foot to release the soil, and laying it all the same way down the row. Other children were organised to come behind the pickers and tie it into bundles. It was easy work to lissome youngsters like us, and I remember that we thoroughly enjoyed ourselves all the day long. We sat in groups in the hedgerow at luchbreak, drinking our lemon squash and eating cucumber sandwiches already curling up, and the boys eyed the girls and the girls giggled amongst themselves, eating daintily in contrast to our wolfish behaviour. When the day ended, the field was all but cleared, and the pleased farmer gave us all three shillings each for the six hours' work we had each given him. That was better money than for potato picking. We were delighted.

Wednesday, August 26th. Fine day. Went flax picking all day. We got 5/6 each for picking. Mr Bigg gave me 10/- for my share of the foxglove leaves and for turning them. Eric Turner moved to Penfedw for good. After flax picking played with the boys up the x-roads.
Tuesday, 1st Sept. Fine Weather. Went getting foxglove leaves in the afternoon. In the evening went down Ffynone to show Mrs Edwards my paintings. Got hers and Mrs Daniels autographs. Went to Chapel after. Archibald our hen was killed.

———————

We lay on our bellies on top of one of the crossroad hedges, watching two ladies of obvious wealth (they had chiffon scarves around their necks) searching about in the grass verge, their car close by. They had lost something of importance, we guessed. We clambered over the hedge and approached them, leaping poles at the ready. They were quite old, in their thirties; they had lost a ring. We helped them search, but without luck.

111

Eventually they reluctantly left, but not without giving us their address. Miss Miller,
Llanfair,
Llandyssul, Cardigan.
When they had gone, I decided to run home and get our wooden rake. Within minutes of using it, we caught a tiny shimmer, and found a small, exquisite ring blinking at us. I can still recall the tremendous shout of triumph we gave, the ecstasy, and the war-dance. Eirlys found a small box for us, and she was as excited as we as she lay it in some soft white paper. She said, 'There's lovely, isn't it?' We posted the ring to Miss Miller by registered post, and within three days the lovely lady had sent us a reward, which amounted to eleven shillings each—an unexpected fortune. By the standards of the day we were quite rich youngsters. It all went into National Savings.

Saturday, Sept 26th. Lovely weather. In the morning took my clogs down to Abercych for nailing. In the afternoon Cyril Fathers and I brought all the leaves down from Pentre on my truck to Newchapel. In the evening I took them all to Boncath on the bus, and waited there, and came back with Megan on the bus afterwards.
Wednesday, Oct 7th. Fair weather. Went down Abercych in the morning and got my glogs—new woods. In the afternoon Megan and Mr Thomas and I picked our spuds at Cilrhiwfach. In the evening played with Waggy and Eric then went to the Reading Room.

For days Hen Griff the carpenter had been making a waggon wheel, a marvellously intricate work which came up to my head when it stood upright in his shed. Dai y Gof—the blacksmith—had been up and measured the rim which he encircled with a miniature wheel, chalking the start mark and counting the number of revolutions. It looked easy, until we heard the words 'overlap' and 'shrinkage'. The day had now arrived when both carpenter and blacksmith were to combine their crafts and fit the tyre to the wheel, at the momentous hour of six in the evening. Mr Griffiths rolled the wheel down to the forge, and we all gathered around. Muriel and her brother John had laid

112

out a line of water buckets. The wheel was laid on the huge ring of stone outside the forge, and hub secured. Dai y Gof, with the assistance of Muriel, brought out the tyre directly off the forge fire, both of them gripping the red rim with large clamps, and even as they moved to the wheel the red began to fade to purple. With the utmost precision they laid the tyre fair to the wheel rim. Smoke and sizzling ensued and we cooed in wonder. Dai y Gof and Muriel had each picked up a hammer, she was a smaller one than her father's, and they beat down the tyre with mighty, methodical blows, walking slowly round as they did, and we counted out the time in rhythm, caught up in the act, so to speak, for it was a wonderful thing to watch. When the tyre was on fair and square, down went the hammers and John and Hen Griff poured on the water quickly and evenly, so that the steam rose in white clouds that died almost as soon as they were formed, and the hissing stopped. All stood back, the job completed, the wheel tyred to perfection, for us to look at and admire, and that was the only time I ever saw a fourteen year old girl wield a hammer with such commitment and strength. There was no denying the pleasure that Muriel felt, and as she stood in her ankle socks and clogs and heavy skirt, hands on hips, chest heaving, there was not one of us who did not sense her superiority. Her arrogance towards us was evident. By comparison we were puny. Muriel had little charm. She had a man's body, a man's legs and arms. But on that evening it was these attributes which made her quite special, above all of us. It was really Muriel's evening.

The wheel slab was also used when one of the villagers had a pig killed. On it the carcass would be laid, as if in sacrifice to the gods, and everybody joined in with scraper and hot water to denude the white body of its hairs. Then the salting began, with legs severed and body cut open, and the bits hung up out of the way in the dairy, or some other cold place. It was almost a social occasion.

Saturday, October 10th. Fine weather. Dug and finished our potatoes at Cilrhiwfach in the morning. In the afternoon Waggy and Eric and I went down TiGoch way and got conkers. In the evening we went getting nuts and we got 4½lbs. Went to the reading room then.

On Sunday, October 11th, the harvest festival was held at Carregwen, and we set out with water-plastered hair and shining shoes to try and get a seat next to the girls. It was the custom to set out benches on the grass at the rear of the church if the weather was fine, and so it was possible to choose where one sat. As it happened, we managed to get a bench in front of the Edwards girls. All around there was the abundance of harvest, sheaves of wheat and barley, marrows, apples and great nebulae of flowers, and they hid the box which was the altar for this service.

I smirked continually at Dorothy over my shoulder, and I was pleased to see her laughing behind her hymn book. I was quite under the impression that I was doing well, actually captivating her, until Eric whispered that the seam in my trousers had split and the girls could see the white of my pants. It was a sobering experience from then on, and I sat up straight so that my bottom revealed less of the split which I was certain gradually inched wider and wider. When we stood up to sing I self-consciously clenched my cheeks together.

Horseflies determined which girls we would accompany after services at Carregwen. These vicious insects inhabited one particular lane in swarms, and when we entered this lane we rolled our socks up to our knees and tried to pull our trousers down to cover our socks, and stretched our jacket sleeves so that our hands were protected. Then we ran shouting the three hundred yards from the top of the lane to the bottom, only a few minutes from the Lawless girls' house. Therefore, if the horseflies were out marauding in vast numbers, we returned the Pentre way and accompanied the Edwards girls. If we emerged unscathed from the lane, we hung on to the front gate of the Lawless house.

Monday, October 12th. Got a smaller uniform at Crymmych. Dull day. Started school again. Planted our onion sets in the garden in the evening before Cadets.

We attended meetings once a week at the dull village of Crymych, which nestled on the slopes of Frenni Fawr. It was a long walk, but only a short car ride. Mr Williams, the head-master of Blaenffos school, automatically promoted to Officer in Charge, Cadets, collected us in his Morris. By the time he had picked up his troops at Capel Newydd, and Boncath, and Blaenffos, his Morris was above the legal loading limit, but I can never remember seeing a policeman to point this out to him. He was small and friendly, a kind, walrus-faced man, flat-footed, who undertook his training programme very seriously. Because of his flat feet his marching and drill demonstrations, carried out with a manual under his arm, were rather untidy but we forgave him. The manual never left his possession, for he constantly referred to it and then taught us. We had no weapons, only sticks, but there was an old Lee Enfield allocated to us, which we dismantled and reassembled and fired and cleaned with a pull-through and oil. There was also a modern .22 rifle, and sometimes we finished drill early in order to take this weapon out to the fields and fire real bullets at rabbits.

Our unit was about twenty in number, fairly equally divided between Welsh and English. We excelled at Fieldcraft. Much later, when taking a Proficiency Test, I ended up not two yards from the invigilating Captain (my small frame cocooned in netting and ferns) and I heard the Captain say to Mr Williams, 'Where have the little buggers got to now?' And wise Mr Williams answered, 'Well, sir, one of them is about to dust your shoes.'

Wednesday, Nov 18th. Fine weather. Cold. A big Service was held all day at Chapel and dinner and tea held. I went to the tea. In the evening Waggy and Eric and I built a bridge down the Outlaws Wood. Letter from Mum, also wrote back. Lost this Diary in the Lodge wood but found it tomorrow. Went to the Reading Room.

Autumn had come and gone, having lingered for many weeks in a blaze of gold and red. It had been a wonderful year for hazel nuts, and we spent much of our time down Cilgwyn woods. Here we could explore places we had never seen before despite our numerous excursions. There were at least two haunted houses, crumbling ruins of brick and stone, sullen piles half hidden by undergrowth. We approached them with exaggerated stealth, for one never knew when Mr Davis the gamekeeper might pop up. And there was an odd woman down

115

there, the wife of one of the farmworkers, a hugely fat woman who stood outside her cottage and laughed helplessly whenever she caught sight of us.

Mr Thomas had told me that there was gold in the river down in these woods. High quality gold, but so little of it in so much stone that it wasn't worth mining. 'Mind you,' he said as an afterthought, 'for each little piece you bring me you shall have a bar of chocolate.' So when we arrived at the river we invariably waded along it in our wellies, peering under stones, digging at the small mudbanks with our swords or leaping poles, hoping to catch the glitter of the fabled gold. In the summer evening we paddled along the stream in bare legs, which in time brought one past Ffynone and through Abercych and into unknown country.

As the autumn colours lost their brilliance, became drab, then faded altogether, we tended to keep to the Outlaws Wood, just a few hundred yards away, where most of our secret huts were, and the Lodge Wood at the bottom of the village street which was a constant source of firewood. A wonderful place for scouting and tracking, for the ground was thick with pine needles. Once, I saw two badgers scuttle by me, and in the permanent twilight of that silent wood they did not see me. As winter drew closer, the Lodge wood became more and more our rendezvous; we welcomed its dry floor, and the silence, the thermal feel of it. It was a winter's wood.

Thursday, Dec 10th. Terrible weather, rain. Only four of us at school, so had an easy day. Made Xmas Cards in school. In the evening Mrs Thomas and I brought 2 live hens back from Yetwen. We also plucked two up there.

Wednesday, Dec 16th. Rotten weather. Rain all morning. Letter from Mum, wrote back, and to Joke Editor, and Grandad. In the evening went collecting with Elfyn Lewis for the Bible Society and we got 19/3d. Fluff our cat was drowned because of her bad foot.

December 25th. Friday. Darlan the Admiral of the French Fleet was assassinated. Rotten weather. Drizzle all day. Had lots of presents. Stayed in all day.

A quiet Christmas Day. We had no visitors, and we visited no one. We had had a tremendous Christmas Eve Party at Ffynone

116

again, but I had missed Donald. And now I missed Frank and Donald, for on this day we could probably have paid quick visits to each other and shown off our presents. Mr Thomas watered the immense fern in its pot in the front room and then had a snooze, and Eirlys thumped at the piano and sang her favourite hymns. Mrs Thomas knitted and talked, and I read my books and ate sweets, while Megan tidied up her bedroom and kept popping up and downstairs. It was exactly like a Sunday. Had there been sunshine we would have gone out for a bike ride, possibly even to Newcastle Emlyn to see Aunt Liz.

> *Saturday, December 26th. Glorious day. In the morning played up the Penfordd woods with Eric and Waggy. In the afternoon we went to to the Cilrhiwfach Auctioneering Sale at Yetwen, but we boys played rugger in the field by there.*
>
> *Thursday, December 31st. Lovely weather. Cold. In the morning got sticks in Penfordd wood with Don Bigg, Eric and Waggy. In the afternoon we went exploring down Cwmfelyn and had fun with Mrs Davies's goat. Reading Room in the evening.*

Presents for Christmas, 1942.
    Mother. Two hankies. Saving Card with four 6d stamps in it.
    A diary, sweets, 2/- and 2/6 from Grandad.
    Megan. A box of sweets.
    Eirlys. Box of sweets and two apples and an orange.
    Mrs Thomas. Four hankies.
    I was happy and satisfied with my lot. My finances were in sound condition, for I had earned 53/6d, 13/6d up on the previous year, and this did not include carol singing earning. I was quite a rich young man.

My new diary cost 3/8—my mother had forgotten to erase the price.

> *January 1st, 1943. Friday. Dull weather. Went to Chapel Tea in the afternoon. Good fun. Wrote to Dai. Went out saying Happy New Year.*

This was a quaint custom which I sometimes think began in Capel Newydd and ended there. One wrapped up well before setting out at first light, or even in the dark hours, to knock at all the houses where it would be reasonably certain someone would answer. A thump on the door and then the plaintive chant in Welsh which roughly translated said. 'Happy New Year, and a present, please.' The good people upon whom we inflicted ourselves at this unearthly time of day usually gave us threepence, or 6d, sometimes a Welsh cake too. They preferred the caller to be dark and handsome, therefore I set out with a double disadvantage. Nonetheless, I was treated always with a smile and on more than one occasion was given a swift kiss and a pat on the curls for luck by people with more sense than to think that only dark callers could bring them luck.

The tempo of our lives did not change substantially. We went to school, we worked in the gardens of our billets, we played up the cross roads and in the endless acres of woods, we had sword fights in the hedges, we attended church and chapel, and our evenings were spent at the Reading Room. And the Cadet Force occupied one evening a week. There was not much time for relaxing.

> *January 29th, Friday. Fine weather. In the evening we acted our play at Capel Colman. It went well. I had a book off the Reverend Jones called 'Buckingham Palace.' Ugh.*

Eric Thomas's sister Beryl, a Sunday school teacher, had rehearsed us for the play. When the first and only night arrived the Parish room was crowded. I recall that we nearly all forgot our lines but made a splendid effort at improvisation, which fooled everybody except Beryl.

The Reverend Jones was rector of the isolated little church of Capel Colman, stuck out in the fields at the back of Cilwendeg as if rejected by the Almighty. He was a scholarly person, slender as a thumbstick, with a thin pointed nose, and silver spectacles perched on the bridge of it. He had none of the fire of our chapel preachers, none of the warmth of our own Reverend Rogers, a real minister. We did not know of the cross he had to bear. Or rather, we knew his wife was very ill, but it never occurred to us that this could make him the sombre person who inflicted such dull sermons on the ear.

118

We first saw the ailing Mrs Jones when we began rehearsals in the Parish Room at the rear of the rectory. As we trudged up the gravel drive, kicking a stone amongst us, we were aware of her. She was a white, ravaged face at the window of the lounge, raised on an arctic of high pillows on a bed in the bay, and as we paused half in shock at seeing her she smiled at us and waved a thin arm in greeting, in slow motion, as if the gesture required all her strength. We waved back, and from then on we waved whenever we saw the window, knowing that she could see us.

The Reverend Jones took half a dozen of us for Confirmation classes, which we bore stoically, and on April 8th we were confirmed by the Bishop of St David's at St Mary's church, Cardigan.

Friday, April 30th. Fine weather. Worked in the garden all morning. Explored the Cwmfelyn Mill in the afternoon with Waggy and Eric. Went back in the evening and brought back two bike wheels for my truck.

Monday, May 3rd. Dull weather. Started school again, and we are now in the Parish Room. In the evening went salvaging with my new truck and got a sackful.

If there are indeed turning points in one's life, where one can quite specifically say, 'at this point I was affected, and my life was changed,' then this was one. I was not immediately aware of it, of course. But this day marked the end of a period in our young lives, for in going to the Parish Room we left behind us a part of childhood. We lost our beautiful, friendly hedges, those humming battlefields of sycamore and ash and beech where we hid and fought whenever we could, free milk in one hand, sword of hazel in the other. There were hedges all around us even now, but none with the vastness and secret places like those of Cilgwyn lane. That area was now deprived of our triumphs, our stampedes and battle cries, our marble competitions and truck rides. The village too, was diminished by our transfer to the Parish Room. The harsh reality of economics had dictated that the Reading Room could not be kept as a school for only eleven pupils—the others having gradually drifted back to Hythe—and therefore there had to be an amalgamation of Boncath and Capel Newydd, at a halfway house—the Parish Room.

> *Thursday, May 6th. Fine weather. In the evening I worked in the garden then improved my truck. Mrs Reece y Gof not very well.*
> *Friday, May 14th. Fair weather. Our salvage was taken away. We had 8cwts of books. We hoed a bit of the school garden. In the evening went to Cadets at Boncath.*
> *Thursday, May 20th. Fair weather. Wrote to Mum. In the evening I attended a Wings for Victory Parade in the village.*

The Parade was held at the back of the Ffynone Arms, in the small sloping field that was spotted with cow pats every day of the week. Our local Home Guard arrived in splendour, out-shining the units from Boncath and Blaenffos and Cilgerran because they were on home ground and had made a special effort to look the part of fighting men. We totalled about forty, altogether. Then came a squad of Americans, the first we had ever seen, and they looked very ordinary in their soft uniforms, despite auroras of chevrons and medals. One of the Boncath men had us in fits when he said of the bemadalled American Captain, 'I hear they get a medal for going to the toilet after dark!' When they stood at ease, the Americans sagged in the middle. Captain Williams prowled up and down our ranks muttering 'show them what you can do, you men.' A padre read out some solemn notes, we sang a hymn, there was a minute's silence, a short sermon which we found difficult to hear because of the noise of the wind, then we marched from the field, down the lane, past the Ffynone Arms where a Colonel took the salute next to the pump, and up past the Reading Room and into Cilgwyn field. There, we dispersed. I thought that the girls from the village and far off would flirt around us, since we had marched so well, but to my astonishment, and that of my friends, they were all over the Americans, laughing with them, and getting autographs and chewing gum. We slunk off.

The following Saturday we had a Sports Day, a new event in the village curriculum. A large crowd was expected, so the top field was to be used, and Mr Evans the Tavern had removed his cattle from it the previous day. We boys had been looking forwards to this event for some time, and had practised with our leaping poles clearing the higher farm gates. We did not bother to practise at running or jumping, quite confident that there would be no opposition. And as for the cycle race—well, it would be no contest—look how we 'spitfired' about on our borrowed bikes. Four of us were entering, and the only worry was who was going to come fifth.

There were the usual events, vaulting, high jump, long jump, standing jump, the hundred yards, the quarter mile, the cycling quarter mile, throwing the grenade (a new one), the marathon as a Special Treat, and sack racing for the children. A full day. A track encircling the field was marked by binder twine on stakes, and a judge's tent had been erected. There were two or three Fete Stalls, run by a gaggle of church and chapel ladies, with nothing on them to interest us athletes.

On this day we wore plimsoles and shorts, and we mingled with the white-skinned farmworker athletes, whose arms were brown from the elbows down so that from a distance they looked dismembered, and their legs were white and blue-veined and knobbly-muscled. They nearly all wore boots. We glanced at them covertly, these would be runners and jumpers, and honestly, they were a joke! We were going to have to take care that we did not offend anyone with our wins—it was a good job that there weren't cash awards!

There were elimination races in the cycle events. One by one the four of us were eliminated. I had borrowed Eirlys' bike, a light machine, but it made no difference and I was fairly beaten. I failed to appreciate the stamina and ruthless determination of our Welsh opponents. They were going to compete against each other, and no bloody evacuee was going to get in the middle. I bounced through the molehills and slithered in the cowpats with some style, but with just a quarter of the race covered I was panting hard, almost at the back of the field, and at least ten bikes of all sizes and shapes had bounced and rattled past me, with their riders grimly leaning over handlebars. I suffered the double indignity of coming last and covered in spots of cow dung. 'There's something wrong with the steering,' I told Waggy by way of an excuse, but I knew that he did not believe a word of it.

121

Only a specially selected group of athletes were permitted to enter the marathon. They were hard-muscled, nervous men as they crouched by the start line, grinning at the crowd and at each other. Then they were loping off, down towards Cilgwyn and the cwm, up the fields of the far side of the valley and round Bwlch y Groes and back. They would be away for sometime, so the sports continued. I won the wheelbarrow race, with Cyril Fathers as handler, and was given a marrow. Great, I though wryly, I grow them! We threw the grenade, but lost to John and Muriel. 'I thought you had to throw it *between* the posts, not as far as you could *beyond* them,' I complained to Muriel, hoping to give her the impression that I could have beaten her. She just looked at me with pity.

We had eagerly awaited the Leaping Pole event. I remember a young fellow a couple of years older than us, with a very long pole of ash. I knew by the way he flexed his hands and held the pole that he was the one to watch. I failed to see the other three fellows who came second, third and fourth. The winning leap was seven feet two inches, a phenomenal height. The highest of our farm gates was barely five feet, and we thought that would be sufficient to win. We were not doing at all well. The running races followed the same pattern. We were no match for these people. Still, they were older than us. In another year or so we'd show them . . .

The marathon men dribbled back into the field and round the perimeter, and they looked as though they really had run twenty six miles instead of about seven. They were greeted at the Finishing line like heroes, and the winner was presented with a small pig, and there was clapping for a long time as the tail-enders came in. It was a splendid end to our Sports Day. The Ffynone Arms was a noisy place that evening.

Tuesday, May 25th. Fine weather. Mrs Rees Y Gof almost dying. In the evening did some weeding, then went down Cilrhiwfach hill on my skates truck.
Wednesday, May 26th. Mrs Rees died. Letter and 2/- from Mum. Went to Cadets in the evening. I saw a badger in the bottom spinney.

Poor Mrs Rees. Very fat, small, thick glasses, and always aproned. Muriel's mother, wife of Dai y Gof, English by birth.

She had never been a talkative person, and though the Forge
Cottage was opposite us I seldom saw her standing and
chatting as the other women of the village seemed to do. I don't
think I spoke more half a dozen words to her. Nevertheless, she
was liked. There was nothing about Mrs Rees to dislike, and
when she quietly passed away on that late spring evening, the
village was silent with sorrow for her and the family she left
behind. John was a year younger than us, and we felt for him.

> *Saturday, June 5th. Fine weather. Worked in the garden all
> afternoon then went and played with Cyril. We had a darn
> good talk on Pentre haystack.*

Haystacks were excellent places in which to have darn good
talks, for they are private places, set apart from the rest of the
farm, and one can relax in any posture with the utmost
comfort. Cyril and I had decided we would go to Canada,
where our talents would be appreciated. He could draw his
cows and I would paint ships. We vowed to start saving, and he
gave me sixpence to put in a tin which we would hide in a cavity
in the stone wall of Brynawel Stores. I promised to add my own
sixpence to it. It was a good start. In 1972 I retrieved the tin and
the 3/8d it contained, and gave Cyril back his half. Somehow,
our paths had diverged.

> *Tuesday, June 8th. Fair weather. In the evening worked in the
> garden then went and cut some peasticks. Mr Wooldridge died.*

Another villager had gone the way of all flesh. It was sad, for
he was not yet fifty, but had suffered 'from the dust' for many
years. Now there were two boys in the village with only one
parent. The Wooldriges and the Reeses lived next door to one
another, and it was almost as if that pair of little white-washed
cottages on the foxgloved bank had a strange curse over them.

> *Thursday, June 10th. Broke up for Whitsun Hols. In the
> evening worked in the garden then played with the boys. Wrote
> to Mum. Mrs Thomas brought me a pair of overalls.*

It seemed that all I had to offer to the world was an aptitude
for gardening, for I had, under the firm tutelage of Twm

123

Llewellyn, become very good at it. For two years now I had dug and raked, weeded and sown and planted and hoed that incredibly fertile garden that was his passion. He was a special teacher and I think I was possibly a special pupil. I never tired of the garden, and often went out and did jobs that I thought ought to be done. I also had my own little patch at the bottom on which I grew cucumbers and marrows, and sold them. Digging fascinated me. Twm Llewellyn had told me long ago that any fool could turn soil over, but only real gardeners knew how to do it properly so that all the hollows were filled in, and all the weeds were entrenched deep out of sight, to do their job of enriching the soil. We were already well on course for the Llechryd Show, where most of his trophies had been won outright. Between us we grew carrots twenty seven inches long, onions sixteen-and-a-half inches in circumference, parsnips thirty nine inches long, all of supreme quality, grown without trickery. We did everything with quiet pride. Sometimes, after a particularly good evenings work, he would give his lovely smile and thump me gently on the arm and say, 'Hey, Dick bach, they're champions already and not half grown!' Sometimes, too, Mrs Thomas or Eirlys would worry at the length of time we stayed out in the garden, and one or the other came trotting along the path to say that we'd done enough and it was late and everyone else was thinking of bed.

So when Mrs Thomas told me of the overalls, I quite thought they were to wear in our garden. I was in for a revelation.

My verse for chapel this evening was rather complex, 'In the beginning there was the Word, the Word was with God, and God was the Word.' All in Welsh. I sat in the fork of my favourite tree up the crossroads, the one with the branch about five feet from the top of the hedge, so that you had to leap out into space to grab it, then swing yourself along it and into the bole of the tree. It was a good Test. So there I was, surrounded by the bright green leaves of late Spring, and the birds singing their evensong. I had my Testament Newydd perched on my drawn-up knees, and I recited the verse over and over. It was important that I got things right for tonight's preacher. He was a lay preacher from over the hill and had had tea with one of the village families prior to attending chapel. It was the custom for someone to offer the travelling preachers sustenance in this way, and they all took it in turns.

I heard a slow, measured stride approaching, a creak-groan, creak-groan. The unmistakable sound of boots, shiny boots, and on parting the leaves saw the preacher, tall and straight in dark suit and dark hat, hands clasped behind him. I kept my eyes on him, smirking at my advantage. It would be a reversal of roles later on, when I would be a little afraid of his presence, for they were men of fierce belief and loud voice, who had a message to bring. We were all sinners.

He slowly strode on to the little triangle of grass to the left of the crossroads, and stood there, stork-like. He looked up towards Yetwen, behind him to the top school, to his left in the direction of Abercych, and to his right, Capel Newydd, from whence he had come. He and I were the only humans on earth. He seemed to sag a little, flex his legs. And then I heard, to my utter disbelief, the sharp staccato of flatulence. Greatly relieved, he straightened himself to his customary pose and walked pensively back towards the village. When he had passed under my tree I jumped down, crossed the road and sped down to the village, and told Waggy and one or two of the other boys what I had witnessed, which caused great whoops of glee. I told Twm Llewellyn, and he too shook in mirth but told me not to mention it to the ladies as they might be offended. 'We're all humans, Dick bach,' he reminded me with a wide grin. From that evening on I regarded the preachers with less awe. The secret was out—they *were* humans.

Our own chapel minister was Mr Rogers, whom we all loved and respected. He often sat with us for a Sunday tea, and like me adored Mrs Thomas's apple pie with cloves, done to a deep brown in the oven. He wrote in my autograph book. (The future lies before you, like a sheet of driven snow. Be careful how you tread it, for every step will show.') When he gave his sermon, he had an endearing habit of underlining the import-ance of a passage by repeating it in Enlgish, sometimes just for my benefit as often I would be the only English person in the congregation. And one such pearl of wisdom has remained in

125

my mind forever. 'It is better to light a candle than to walk in darkness.' He was a very good advertisement for chapel.

Saturday, June 12th. Fine weather. Did odd jobs in the morning. In the afternoon we cycled up to Herman to see the Sports. Spent 1/6 but didn't win anything. Mr Wooldridge was buried.
Wednesday, June 15th. Back to school. Went to Cadets in the evening. News that I have a job up Cilwendeg.
Friday, June 18th. Rotten day. MY LAST DAY AT SCHOOL. Painted a picture in the evening. Mrs Thomas's Birthday.

I do not recall my state of mind on finishing school at the age of fourteen. There were so few of my age group left that little remained to be said. I would like to think that Mr Bigg felt grief at my departure, but he probably felt relief. I remember returning *Mungo Park* and thinking that that would be the last book on Africa I would read for a long time, little knowing . . . Had there been a larger class I think the opinion of those responsible for our welfare may well have suggested that I keep on at school, but as things were, there were only a few twelve and thirteen years old remaining. My mother had decided that I was quite happy where I was, and had fallen in with Mrs Thomas's suggestion (no doubt vigorously backed by Twm Llewellyn) that I get a job, and where better than in the garden of a Great House like Cilwendeg? My apprenticeship would be the best available, the best in Britain, and that meant the best in the world. I was lucky 'they' were willing to have me, as not everyone met the standards required by Daniel Daniels, Esq. Gentleman, J.P. Oh, yes, he owned Cilwendeg, too!

My boyhood was over. On Monday I would be a Man.

It was with no small degree of uncertainty and apprehension that I presented myself to Griff y Gardd on Monday morning of June 21st, in brand new bib and brace and gasmask case crammed with midmorning sandwiches, and bottle of cold sweet tea, and my clogs freshly Dubbined.

I knew Mr Davis—Griff y Gardd (Griff of the garden)—only by sight, and thought I'd probably like him, which was to

126

prove true. I was not so sure of Evans y Lodge—the under-gardener, for he had been Waggy's billetor, and seemed a morose character. I'd once planted five hundred lettuce plants for him and he'd blamed me for their curling up and dying, so we didn't really speak to each other. Now, here I was, under him, for eight hours a day. He greeted me civilly enough, I recall.

Mr Davis didn't beat about the bush. He told me he knew that I could do most of the things that needed doing, but he'd show me round the garden first.

Cilwendeg Garden was magnificent, entirely given over to vegetable crops, but there were thickets of fruit shrubs, and fruit trees lined all the immaculate paths. It was split into two parts, with the top part given over to glasshouses and neat plots between them. The second half, beyond a high wall, was two very large pieces of cultivated ground measuring forty paces square each. At the very end of this part of the garden was another wall pierced by a small archway. We didn't go into this, but I was told it was a yew maze with a pond, a relic of the great days, left alone on Daniel Daniels' instructions. The yew was slow growing and poisoned the ground so that weeds did not grow, and the pond could look after itself.

To my surprise, Mr Davis sent me out to the back of the garden to cut myself a small hazel fork, a miniature thumbstick, about ten inches long. My first job. With this instrument he then began to demonstrate how to shape a grape bunch. Evans y Lodge was already at work doing a bunch. I had never seen grapes growing before. Mr Davis pointed to the grapes, telling me which ones ought to be removed. He gave me my hazel fork and left me to it. 'I'll be back in an hour,' he told me. 'But don't you do just that bunch, now then. When you've finished you watch Mr Evans.' So, it was going to be surnames. In the event I was still busy at my bunch when Mr Davis returned. 'Now, Dick bach,' he said. 'This is your bunch. You'll know it because your fingertips will be all over the bloom, just like you buy in the shops. Here, we do things properly. First, the scissors . . .'

He showed me how to shape the bunches, using the hazel fork to lift up the stems, the scissors to cut off all the inside

127

grapes, and using my eye like an artist, to cut and shape as I went up the bunch. There would be nothing inside, but the outside grapes would be huge and beautiful to see; like chandeliers, the bunches would be.

On that first day I shaped three bunches on the enormous grapevine. Mr Evans and I spoke infrequently, and Mr Davis popped in and out, always busy. I went home for lunch, up the side of Cilgwyn field, through the spinney hedge and into our backway, a ten minutes' journey. I was impatient to continue my demanding job, to Mrs Thomas and Eirlys's delight. 'Duw, there's a good start, eh?'

I went back early, for I wished to see the yew maze and the pond. I ran to the end of the garden and through the archway, into a damp and cool area, another world from the hot garden on the other side of the wall. The swimming pool for such it was, was round, about twenty feet in diameter. The water winked greenly and I saw a frog clinging to a piece of debris, regarding me wisely. I resolved to visit here again.

The first few days were idyllic. I loved the work, almost felt guilty that Mr Davis was doing all the necessary watering. My skill increased so that I was able to complete about six bunches a day. Then Mr Davis told me that I'd learned enough about grapebunch shaping—I'd never forget how to do it for the rest of my life, and I was being paid to learn, too.

Saturday, July 10th. Had my first pay. £3.4.0. Went to Town with Cyril in the afternoon.

Eric of the old Ffynone Gang had gone back to Hythe on June 25th, and now I was the sole survivor, a wage-earning man. I had passed my Certificate 'A' in the cadets, which ensured the Germans a tough passage should they ever land. And Waggy began work at Ffynone Garden on July 12th.

We had our Saturday afternoons free, and met up to go to town, or wander down the dingle. We no longer used our skate truck, that was for kids, and the weapons of childhood had been discarded. Our hands were becoming hard, men's hands, our voices had broken, mine reluctantly, and we had become a little more circumspect.

July 23rd. Lovely weather. In the evening I cycled to Newcastle Emlyn with Eirlys and had a short stay with Aunt Liz. Went to Cenarth Falls and saw the salmon leaping the Falls. Wednesday, July 28th. Fine weather. Went up 'cadets' at Crymych in the evening. HAD MY L/C STRIPES.

Waggy and I met again at Ffynone, for I was seconded to the farm for haymaking. We now had a pitchfork each, and worked as hard as the other men, with no favours offered. After all, we were getting wages. I could not help thinking that things really were very good indeed. Here we were, doing what we'd always liked doing, but getting paid for it.

On August 7th I had my annual holiday, already arranged by the Cadet Force on my behalf. We had a week at Pendine, on an Army camp, during which time we learned to shoot real bullets and all were shaken by the noise a Lee Enfield made. The weather was poor, the food worse, and if anything was designed to put us off the Army, that week succeeded. I was roped in for a boxing bout, my opponent being a dancing little Welshman from Cardiff, and we beat hell out of each other in the name of our respective units. It was a draw. I think that I resolved at Pendine that the Army was not for me. This was too much like the real thing.

By mid August Waggy and I were once again at Ffynone, involved with the corn harvest.

Friday, August 20th. Rotten weather. In the afternoon we cleared out the river bed so that the water went the right way. Took a message to Penfeddw. Concert in the Reading Room.

The work at Cilwendeg was not in the least hard yet. All the digging had been done. At this time of the year there were the pleasant tasks to do, hoeing, picking, watering. The mansion itself was part of a Ministry, housing quite a number of Important Civil Servants, who came in dribs and drabs down to the garden on Saturday mornings to buy fresh produce, and I thought they were all spies and decoders. On Friday mornings I took up to the kitchen a truck of produce. The cook and her assistant always accepted the produce through an open window—I was never allowed inside. On the first morning I went there, the cook looked me over as I handed her the lettuce and other things, and she said to her friend, never dreaming that I could understand. 'Here Ruth, Here's a pretty boy for you.' 'Bachgen hyfryd!' On Monday mornings it was also my job to rattle along Cilwendeg drive with the truck and wait at the bus stop with the produce. The passengers always stared hard as it was being loaded underneath in the luggage area, and it occurred to me what a good idea it would be to advertise where it all came from. I made the suggestion to Mr Davis but it did not appeal to him. He thought our freight charge would go up from 3d a tray to 6d.

We had wonderful strawberries that year, lying on beds of straw so that they would not get the mould. I was told to eat when I liked as I would soon get used to them, and that was better than trying to hide them under my jumper. That went for all the fruit. 'I don't want any stealing or hiding,' I was told. 'If you want an apple or a pear, pick it and eat it!' I have often thought what wise advice that was, because I discovered that where there was no challenge there was no real reason to pick —I only felt like having the odd apple once in a while. Had the picking of them been forbidden I would have wanted to pick an apple all day. Our grapes were magnificent. Mr Davis pointed out my bunch with the fingerprinted bloom, and let me have it. When the bunches were cut they were laid out on cabbage leaves in the trays, and I was very proud of them at the bus stop.

> *Tuesday, September 14th. Rotten weather. Rain all day. Went to cadets at Cilgerran in the evening. Killed 80 flies in our kitchen with an elastic band.*
> *Wednesday 15th September. Fine weather. Digging for clay all day in the Outlaws Wood. Stayed in all evening—fed up.*

Mr Davis had told me, 'You've had a very good time up till now, Dick bach, all this picking and hoeing and tying. Griff and I did all the hard work before you came! Him and me's going to have a rest now. I'll show you what you are going to do, now then. Make a man of you this will.'

I trundled a wheelbarrow and spade and fork into the woods, following Mr Davies, who suddenly seemed to be enjoying himself. He had a huge grin on his face, and hummed as he walked flat-footed ahead of me. We arrived at a ravine, about five feet deep. We had often jumped it during our Test—when we were children.

'This,' said Mr Davies, 'is clay. Real, heavy clay. Soon we'll have the old boilers going, and we use *cwlwm* to bank them down for the nights. You know what *cwlwm* is? No? Well, now then, this will be another education for you. *Cwlwm*, Dick bach, is a mixture of clay and coal dust. Dirt cheap, so long as we can dig it ourselves. Or so long as you can dig it for us. We'll start by here,' and he pointed to a part not overgrown by weeds,' and what you do is this. Stand on the edge, and dig out a block with the spade, and just let it fall to the bottom. And as you go along keep it nice and tidy, like. Then you start again, see, and gradually come down. Then you fill the barrow and bring it back to the cellar, and throw it through the window, all ready for you to use. Now then, I'll leave you to it. We'll call you five minutes before lunch so that you can get your clogs cleaned off.' And with that, he was gone, and I was on my own, in my Outlaws Wood, about to ruin it.

It was terribly hard work. I had no idea how difficult and heavy clay was to handle. Chopping it was difficult enough, requiring prolonged effort in just getting the spade to release itself having pierced the stuff. Worse still was the eventual loading of the barrow, for I had to shove the fork into each block and heave it up to the barrow above me. By the time the barrow was loaded I was suffering the first symptoms of utter exhaustion. I had never had to work like this before. And even worse than both the excercise I had just undertaken was pushing the cursed barrow along the wood path, over the little wooden bridge that spanned the stream and up the slope to the cellar wall. We both collapsed at the end of the journey. When I began to select the blocks to heave down through the cellar aperture, they had welded together and I had to chop with my spade again. Finally, I had completed the entire routine, and felt very tired and disheartened. And it was only mid-morning of Wednesday. I had two and a half days more of this, then on Saturday morning I was going to make *cwlwm*.

There was not a single job that I disliked in the garden, and I even got on well with Evans y Lodge insofar that he now spoke to me instead of pointing with his spade and grunting. But what I detested, loathed, was mixing *cwlwm*. From now on, late September, my Saturday morning job was to mix *cwlwm*, enough to last a week. The cellar in which I worked was dark and damp, about twelve feet square. A large pile of coal dust filled one corner, the clay blocks the other. I made a circle of clay blocks, roughly four feet in diameter, and chopped them up, adding water now and again until the clay was a sticky mess, a great porridge. It took me hours of pounding with the spade, a backbreaking job. At the porridge state I then began shovelling coal dust into the mess, turning and chopping, always bloody chopping, until it amalgamated to form a stiff compound, *Cwlwm*. I never see a greenhouse boiler now without recalling the grim Saturday mornings I spent in that cellar at Cilwendeg, praying for twelve o'clock.

One evening, at the very end of that glorious September, it occurred to me that there was one more boyhood act remaining. Time after time I'd quickly scamper to the maze when I was on my own, and take a quick look at the pool. I had discovered that it drained through a pipe in the outside wall, and surmised that in fact the water gradually changed itself over a period of time. I had resolved to have a swim in it. The thought of it fairly took my breath away.

On the last Saturday evening of September I came back to the garden. I shinned up the tree which I had selected for the task, and climbed up it with ease and lay on the top of the garden wall, burying myself in the ivy which grew in profusion along its entire length. I quickly doubled along the wall to the maze section and levered myself down one of the espaliered pear trees, and disappeared into the maze. I was breathless with excitement. I came to the pool and sat down on the concrete path and kicked off my clogs, then my socks, tore off my clothes. Oh, Dorothy, oh, Lois, oh Mrs Thomas and Megan and Eirlys, if only you could see me now! Naked, I lowered myself into the pool. The water was still green, and warm, unbelievably warm. I sank in it up to my chin. I went all round it, half floating, half swimming, with a hand on the edge, and all sorts of soft things underfoot. It was a kind of paradise, far, far exceeding any experience I had imagined. I wanted to stay in it. Caution overcame me, and I hauled myself out and lay gloating and gleaming wet on the concrete again, in the last heat of the evening. It had been the most daring thing I could ever have dreamed up, and I was ecstatic. Boy, what an evening! That moving in the water had been as if I were on a cloud in a green sky, halfway to heaven. There had been nothing in my life to compare with the feel of that mystery pool.

I always told myself that I would visit the pool again, but I never did. That first time was special, and I knew in my heart that it would not be the same a second time. It was a final gesture, a farewell to boyhood, when I stood naked by that pool. We worked the day long, sometimes the pool only yards away, but I never sneaked into the maze to look at it again. I shut myself off, a young man among men now, and although we played down the woods in the late summer evenings, Waggy and Eric and I, the beautiful spirit of boyhood adventure was lost forever. The Outlaws Wood and the Fern Wood and the Top Wood became places where we collected firewood. Nor did we any longer make our forts and barricades in the wondrous hedges. In them we left our broken spears and swords, the apparel of our joyous, innocent years, as we made the transition into young men.

Even the silent, dark and windless spinneys were disappearing, for they were now being devastated by armies of workers with axes. The trees had matured and were now required for pit props. Waggy and I were again seconded to another job, that of assisting in the disposal of the ashes of the great fires that we re-used to burn all the small stuff, and we were even allowed to wield an axe each and lop off the lower branches.

I would whistle for Waggy early in the dark winter mornings, and the two of us clogged our way down the icy road to the Dingle, huddled in our Lease-Lend lumber jackets, resentful, hating the dark and the cold, the prospect of pushing barrow-loads of ash through the mud to Ffynone garden. Men would be standing around the huge mounds of ash, just glowing again after having the corrugated iron sheets removed, and there would be low talk as the men sipped from their aluminium flasks before starting the day's work. Our spirits always rose with the sun, so that by daylight we were our usual happy selves, swapping jokes, discussing the Reading Room and local gossip.

133

Sometimes, at the end of the day, as we trudged back up the hill out of the cwm, we would see the curtain of Mr Lewis the Ffynone head gardener's front room quiver, and know that his daughter Mona was peering at us. A strange, solitary girl, 'not quite the biscuit' as the locals had it, who ran from the garden whenever we appeared.

Once again, at Christmas, we went to the Ffynone Party. The New Year of 1944 came, and with it the endless digging. The days passed as always, every minute occupied with work and Cadets, work and Chapel, work and Reading Room, work and our own garden. We joined the men in the serious business of thrashing the corn, no longer mischievous spectators.

At the age of fifteen we were hard and strong. The odd break from rough work came now and again, but not so often. We had a few weeks sweeping the leaves from Ffynone drive, working with the gentle Mr Lewis, and wished that the job would go on forever.

I worked at Cilwendeg for a summer and a winter and a spring. I scrubbed the fruit trees with a wire brush and carbolic soap and water, learned the art of sculpturing grape bunches, mixed tons and tons of *cwlwm*, and learned that the reward for hard work was satisfaction in a job well done, nothing more nor less.

In that Spring of 1944 the tiny school ceased altogether. Muriel Mawr had a row at home and left to go into service, Twm Llewellyn won more awards at the Llechryd Show, and I wore out my second pair of clogs, and got a Bible for good attendance at Chapel. And I also got my second stripe in the Cadet Force.

In June of that year I went back to Hythe for a short holiday. Eirlys walked as far as Wendros with me, and we kissed goodbye clumsily, and parted, she going back to the quiet, uncomplicated life of Capel Newydd, I into the last phase of the war that had passed us by. I did not return from my short holiday.

I'd had a very good war.

Epilogue

In 1972, my wife and the two girls and I went to Capel Newydd, 340 miles away. At the time, we had a three-wheeler, and the journey took twelve bouncing hours.

Where once I had loped Indian fashion over wide distances, armed with spear or bow and arrow or staff, these distances had been compressed into a small world more lovely than I remembered. The valleys were steeper, the roads narrower and with many more bends, the hills of patchwork fields within hailing distance of each other. We almost passed through Capel Newydd without realising it.

Eirlys seemed not have aged one year. Only she was at the shop now, for both Mr and Mrs Thomas had passed on and Megan, married with a daughter, was living in Anglesey. The spinney of small pines of 1944 at the back of the shop were now tall and heavy, casting an early shadow over the old shop, obliterating the splendid view of Frenni Fawr, so that there was nothing to look at from the kitchen window.

Evans y Beic had long gone, and Hen Griff y Sir, the Thomases of the school house, and the Parrys and Dai y Gof, Griff y Gardd and Evans y Lodge and his wife. But the youngsters of our time had grown up to sustain the community, and I barely recognized them. I would have liked to have seen Alun Wooldridge, but he had left to live elsewhere. My old friends John y Gof and Alun y Tafarn were still there.

Muriel was dying of cancer. She had returned from her maid's job at one of the big houses; come home to die. Muriel Mawr of the massive chest and man's strength, who had towered arrogantly above us in those golden years of our childhood, lay upstairs in her small cottage, wracked with pain. With typical pride and strength, she came downstairs to see my family and me, and I could have wept for her. She was subdued by her suffering, had become gentle. Brave as ever, she smiled all the while we stayed to see her and the rest of her family.

Sarah wanted to post a card as soon as we arrived, so we walked hand-in-hand to the letterbox in the chapel wall. A man was leaning on the wall, looking down at us, a grin on his lean and very brown face. 'About time you visited us, isn't it, then,' he said. I recognized him. Alun Wooldridge's uncle. He had married Mrs Wooldridge, and now they both looked after the chapel and lived in the chapel house. Mrs Wooldridge, still handsome and quick moving and bright, was delighted to see us.

The only addition to the village was a petrol pump near our playfield.

The great houses of Cilwendeg and Pentre had become nests of flats for the aged, secluded and silent as tombs, as if harbouring resentment at the modern age. Ffynone was empty. Eirlys came with us to wander around, and a man who lived in the old chauffeur's flat above the inner yard allowed us into the mansion itself. For me, it was a strange, though not sad, experience to show off our bedrooms and the great kitchen to my family. The lovely old place still had style. The man said that someone from London had plans afoot to change it into a Country Club.

The utter demolition of Cilwendeg garden saddened me immensely. Here, where I spent my first man-hours of labour, where there had been a most marvellous orderliness and a profusion of colours and smells of vegetable and fruit, here was a madness of blackberry and thorn and wild rose, and the gaunt fingers of old greenhouses poking from all that wilderness, as if in condemnation at those who had so neglected it.

We spent an afternoon at Ffynone Dingle. Deep down there, on the way to the waterfall, where marshy ground gave little sighs and the path meandered over fallen logs, we saw a pile of old iron trapped in a profusion of wild rose, almost consumed by nettles. I went over to have a look. I felt a profound sadness as I recognized the shape and old, old colour, the rusted iron seat. It was all that was left of our Fordson Diesel tractor, a poignant symbol of a time remembered.